A Quick Guide to Research Methods for Dissertations in Education

ALSO AVAILABLE FROM BLOOMSBURY

Writing a Watertight Thesis 2nd edition, Mike Bottery, Nigel Wright and Mark A. Fabrizi

Taking Control of Writing Your Thesis, Kay Guccione and Jerry Wellington

Successful Dissertations, edited by Caron Carter

Research Methods for Early Childhood Education, Rosie Flewitt and Lynn Ang

Research Methods for Educational Dialogue, Ruth Kershner, Sara Hennessy, Rupert Wegerif and Ayesha Ahmed

Research Methods for Classroom Discourse, Jenni Ingram and Victoria Elliott

Research Methods for Understanding Professional Learning, Elaine Hall and Kate Wall

Research Methods for Social Justice and Equity in Education, Liz Atkins and Vicky Duckworth

A Quick Guide to Research Methods for Dissertations in Education

Edited by

ABIGAIL PARRISH AND GHAZAL SHAIKH

BLOOMSBURY ACADEMIC
LONDON • NEW YORK • OXFORD • NEW DELHI • SYDNEY

BLOOMSBURY ACADEMIC
Bloomsbury Publishing Plc
50 Bedford Square, London, WC1B 3DP, UK
1385 Broadway, New York, NY 10018, USA
29 Earlsfort Terrace, Dublin 2, Ireland

BLOOMSBURY, BLOOMSBURY ACADEMIC and the Diana logo are trademarks
of Bloomsbury Publishing Plc

First published in Great Britain 2023

Cover design by Grace Ridge
Cover images © DS stories and Jess Bailey Designs / Pexels

A catalogue record for this book is available from the British Library.

A catalog record for this book is available from the Library of Congress.

ISBN: HB: 978-1-3502-6038-2
PB: 978-1-3502-6037-5
eBook: 978-1-3502-6039-9
ePDF: 978-1-3502-6040-5

Typeset by Newgen KnowledgeWorks Pvt. Ltd., Chennai, India
Printed and bound in Great Britain

To find out more about our authors and books visit www.bloomsbury.com
and sign up for our newsletters.

To all our dissertation students, past, present and future

CONTENTS

PART ONE Commonly Used Methods

PART TWO Further Qualitative Methods

FIGURES

TABLES

BOXES

CONTRIBUTORS

Sheikha Al Sheyadi teaches in the English Department at the University of Technology and Applied Sciences, Oman. She has a Doctorate of Philosophy in Education from the University of York, UK and a Masters in teaching and learning methodologies from Mutah University, Jordan. Her research interests focus on Teaching English, Teacher education, Curriculum and instruction and Tertiary education.

Elizabeth Bailey is Senior Lecturer in Education at the University of Lincoln, UK. Her research interests focus on language attitudes, monolingual mindset and multilingualism in educational institutions.

Géraldine Bengsch is Postdoctoral Research Associate at King's College London and Visiting Lecturer at City, University of London, UK. Her research interests include interpersonal and intercultural communication as well as innovative social science research methods. She has published on intercultural identity in society and novel research methods. Her most recent book chapter is 'Using Custom-Built, Small-Scale Educational Solutions to Teach Qualitative Research Literacy: No Code, Code, and Complex Applications' in the *Handbook of Research on Acquiring 21st Century Literacy Skills Through Game-Based Learning* (2022).

Verónica García-Castro is Lecturer and Researcher at Universidad de Costa Rica, Costa Rica, in the Faculty of Education. Her research areas focus on psycholinguistics, L2 language processing, L2 word learning and L2 pedagogy. She has published on word processing and learning. One of her most recent publications is 'The Effects of Vocabulary Knowledge in L2 Semantic Engagement: The Case of Adult Learners of English as a Second Language'.

Asadullah Lashari is Lecturer in English Language and Literature at the University of Sindh, Pakistan. Currently, he is pursuing his PhD from the University of Nottingham, UK. He is also a recipient of the Vice-Chancellor's Scholarship for Research Excellence (International) Award for doctoral studies from the University of Nottingham, UK. His research interests include critical discourse analysis, post-structuralism, feminist post-structural discourse analysis, and leadership and policy analysis.

Kevin McLaughlin is Senior Lecturer in Initial Teacher Development at Bishop Grosseteste University, UK. His research interests focus on the use of social media for professional development opportunities and managing workload in the primary school.

Jelena O'Reilly is Lecturer in Psychology in Education at the University of York, UK. Her research focuses on language, in particular second-language acquisition and child language development. She recently published on the topics of the effects of the home language environment on language development and foreign language anxiety in university students.

Abigail Parrish is Lecturer in Education at the University of Sheffield, UK. Her research focuses on language learning motivation, with a particular interest in school-level language learning. She has published various articles in this area as well as work on intercultural competence. She works with a lot of dissertation students in education.

Jayme Scally is Assistant Professor in the Multidisciplinary Studies Program at West Virginia University, USA. Her research examines issues of social justice within higher education, with emphasis on development of intercultural competencies. She has published on the connection between language and intercultural competence, non-traditional learning formats and supporting international student success. She also served as editor of *Horizons*, an academic journal showcasing the scholarly outputs of undergraduate students.

Ambreen Shahriar completed her PhD in Educational Studies at Goldsmiths, University of London, UK, before joining the University of Sindh, Pakistan, where she taught and supervised a number of research students. Currently, she teaches at University of Northampton, UK. Her research interests include issues of culture and learner identity, multilingualism, multiculturalism, individual learner differences, motivation and research in education.

Ghazal Shaikh is Assistant Professor at Institute of English Language and Literature, University of Sindh, Pakistan. She completed her PhD in Education from the University of York, UK. Her research interests include teaching of citizenship, teaching fiction and teaching citizenship through literature. Her recent work has been published in *Cambridge Journal of Education*, *Asian Journal of Social Science* and *English in Education*.

Hassan Syed is Associate Professor of Applied Linguistics in the Department of Education, at Sukkur IBA University, Pakistan. Currently a postdoctoral fellow at University of Pennsylvania, USA, he obtained his PhD in Education in 2016 from the University of York, UK. He teaches courses, including English pedagogy, educational change and development, research methodology in applied linguistics and education. His research interests are willingness to communicate in a second language, motivational dynamics in the L2 classroom, the role of L1 in the L2 classroom, and teacher research in higher education.

Introduction

Abigail Parrish and Ghazal Shaikh

If you are reading this book, you are probably about to start your undergraduate dissertation in education. Or perhaps you are planning ahead and trying to work out what you might want to do for your dissertation project. Others of you may be part way through, but looking for a resource to help you choose the right method, or understand how a particular method can help you. You're in the right place!

This book is intended to provide a resource you can dip in and out of to help you get to grips with different possible research methods for your project. In our work as lecturers in education, we realized that a simple guide for students to help them understand different research methods and their appropriateness for their chosen dissertation projects was something that was missing, and so we decided to make it ourselves. We worked with wonderful colleagues from around the world who have all contributed chapters on the method of their expertise in an easy-to-follow, user-friendly manner to help you navigate the complexities of research methods.

Some of the most commonly used methods are interviews (or focus groups), questionnaires or observations – or perhaps a combination of two (or even three!) of these methods. This book opens with chapters which explain exactly how you can use them, and when you should and shouldn't choose them. But there are many more options which may not spring immediately to mind but which might be the perfect fit for the project you have in mind. In Parts Two and Three of this book, we explore these other methods in more detail and hope you might think about trying something more unusual if it fits your project.

Whichever method you choose, you need to be aware of the ethical considerations involved in planning your project. Some chapters have specific sections addressing the ethics of using that particular method, but for many methods, and projects, a general understanding of ethics is enough. It is important that you follow your university's ethics procedures to the letter to ensure you don't run into any problems – your lecturers and supervisors will always help with this.

The main thing to be aware of when considering research ethics is that you should not be harming anyone through your research – in fact, you should really be trying to do some good. This may be in the form of direct benefits to your participants, but often, it's about adding to knowledge, even in a very small way.

In order to avoid doing harm to anyone, you need to think about how you inform your human participants about the research and how you give them the information they need to provide you with informed consent. How do they find out what you are asking them to do? How do they know what you will do with their data? What happens if they change their minds about participating? If you are working with young children, do you need to inform their parents, and how will you do this? Are your materials suitable for the group you're working with? All these questions and more come under the umbrella of research ethics, and you should always strive to be as clear and detailed as possible when you fill in your ethical approval paperwork, as required by your university. A good understanding of the research methods you plan to use is a key part of this!

How to Use This Book

Whilst we have tried to gather the chapters together in a logical order, we know that you may not read every one. You may have a good idea of the method you want to use and go straight to that chapter, or you may have a shortlist and want to look through chapters focused on those methods. However, you may be looking for inspiration and want to look through many, or all of the chapters. However you choose to use this book is fine with us – please don't feel you have to read every word or look at each chapter in order! If you do look at more than one chapter, though, you will start to feel at home. The chapters all have a similar structure and common section headings. All of them give you an overview of the method and the key terminology you will need before giving more details about the what, why and how of each method. They also include a note about what the method is not suitable for, to help keep you on the right track. You'll also see that some of the chapters refer to others in this book – that's because there are similarities and areas of cross-over between many of the methods.

Another thing you'll notice as you read different chapters is that we sometimes mention certain software that can help you. We only mention these things in passing as there are plenty of other resources which can give you details of how to download and use them, and you can use the methods we describe without them. Don't be afraid to explore other research methods resources to find out more, though! And don't forget that your supervisors are founts of knowledge when it comes to dissertation projects and can help you design your projects. Other staff at your university, for example library and academic support staff, can also help you, so don't be afraid to ask!

What You'll Find in This Book

Part One covers what we think of as the four most commonly used research methods in undergraduate dissertations in education. In Chapter 1, Ghazal Shaikh explores interviews and looks at how you could design and conduct an interview study and how you would analyse the data you gathered. She introduces us to coding, which is a key part of qualitative data analysis and something you will come across in other chapters as well. In Chapter 2, Elizabeth Bailey looks at focus groups. Focus groups, as you will see, are a kind of group interview which allows you to get the views of groups of people, rather than individuals.

Chapter 3 brings in our first quantitative method. Abigail Parrish explains how we can design and use questionnaires to get data from a bigger group of participants and talks us through some common pitfalls. We are introduced to some quantitative analysis – working with data in the form of numbers rather than words.

In Chapter 4, Géraldine Bengsch looks at observations. If your project is focused on what people do, rather than what they think or feel, observations might be a good method to use, and she helps you to think about when they can be most useful and what you should think about if you choose this method.

In Part Two, we introduce some more qualitative methods. In Chapter 5, Sheikha Al Sheyadi explores document analysis as a qualitative method in education. She explains how different types of texts can be used as data in a dissertation. Chapter 6 introduces us to discourse analysis. Asadullah Lashari talks about analysing spoken and written discourse giving examples of different media of analysis, including conversation and text.

Chapter 7 explains the use of ethnography as a research tool in educational research. Ambreen Shahriar and Asadullah Lashari point out that you can choose to collect data through more than one tool in an ethnographic study. You will use this approach if you are able to go to the research site and have sustained contact with your participants. Data collected is qualitative and analysed using qualitative data analysis techniques.

Chapter 8, 'Netnography', explores the use of the internet as a medium for collecting data for educational research. Kevin McLaughlin examines the possibility of exploring educational research questions using different social media platforms. He gives the example of using Twitter to collect data. The data can be analysed qualitatively using coding, as in interviews.

Chapter 9 is about visual data. Jayme Scally talks about how photographs, movies, maps and symbols can be used as data in educational research. The use of photography, though common in other fields, is relatively new in educational research. The decision to use visual data must be taken carefully in accordance with the research question for the project.

Chapter 10 introduces an innovative method called 'Think-Alouds'. Hassan Syed explains how you can collect data by asking your participants to think aloud while doing your chosen activity. This method is useful if you are interested in the participants' thought process while engaged in an activity. Think-alouds are an advanced qualitative method for which the data is recorded and transcribed and can be analysed through coding.

In Part Three, we look at two further quantitative methods. These are more advanced methods, and the authors explain clearly what type of projects they are suitable for. In Chapter 11, Jelena O'Reilly looks at reaction time methods, focusing on two specific examples: self-paced reading and the Tower of Hanoi puzzle. Because they are so sensitive, reaction time methods are always computer-based tasks, as you will see.

The final chapter focuses on experimental design, and Verónica García-Castro talks us through how an experimental project could allow us to explore areas of classroom practice by creating different conditions for groups of participants. She also introduces us to some more complex qualitative analysis.

Getting Started

Now you know what to expect from the book, it's time to get started! You probably have an idea of the most likely methods you will use, in which case you can start with those chapters. If not, why not begin at the beginning?

PART ONE

Commonly Used Methods

CHAPTER ONE

Interviews

Ghazal Shaikh

What Can They Tell Me?

Interviews are one of the most commonly used methods in educational research. They are used when you are interested in people's perceptions, beliefs or opinions about different topics. We use interviews when 'facts' and numerical data are not enough to answer our research question and when we cannot directly observe what we are interested in. If you think your participants will be able to answer the questions you have for them by engaging in a focussed conversation about the topic, interviews are the method to go for. Interviews enable you to get in-depth data on a one-to-one basis.

Terminology

Table 1.1 explains some key terms that you often hear when using or reading about interviews.

When Might I Use Them?

If you are interested in knowing about the 'challenges faced by teachers in large classes', you could interview a set of teachers who

TABLE 1.1 Interview Terminology

Term	Definition
Interview protocol/ schedule/guide	The set of questions that you prepare before the interview to ask your participants
Pilot	A test run to check whether your instruments are okay to use. You try out your interview schedule with fewer participants to check understandability, time taken and suitability of the questions
Population	All the possible participants for your project
Sample	The participants that you select and collect data from
Coding	The process of naming parts of your data according to the topic being discussed. This process helps organize the data better
Transcribe	Write down word to word the audio recording of an interview
Thematic analysis	Analysis of interview data into codes which then lead to themes

teach large classes in a specific context and ask them what challenges they face. To prepare for your interviews, you will have to prepare an interview guide/schedule. This interview guide will need to be based on your understanding of the context by reading about your area of interest. Your prepared questions could be as follows:

1. What kind of teaching methods do you use while teaching?
2. Do you think there are any positives of having large classes?
3. What are the challenges of teaching literature in these large classes? (Ask for examples from classrooms.)
4. What strategies do you use to overcome these challenges?
5. Do you think it is possible to keep the students active in large classes? How do you do that?

Interviews are a suitable instrument for this study because you are interested in the teacher's views and you want detailed answers.

However, if you were interested in learning about the challenges that the students face while learning in a large class, you would ask the students and your questions would be slightly different.

You might be interested in finding out how the students feel about their interaction with the teacher, their place in the class and engagement with the course content. Possible questions to know about challenges of learning in a large class could be the following:

1. How do you feel about your interaction with the teacher?
2. How do you think your engagement with the course content is affected in a large class?
3. How far do you feel noticed by the teacher and your peers in a large class?
4. What other challenges do you face while learning in a large class?

Interviews help you gain rich, in-depth data. Most interviews are done face-to-face, so you can notice the respondent's facial expressions and body language. This can help to know if the participants have not understood the question or need further explanation, and you can help as and when needed. Sometimes, for practical reasons, some researchers do telephonic or Skype/Zoom interviews as well.

Interviews are used in a variety of topics: for example, if you are interested in knowing readers' perceptions about a specific work of literature. For examples of actual studies using interviews in educational research, refer to Box 1.1.

Box 1.1 Example Studies in Educational Research

Budash, D., & Shaw, M. (2017). Persistence in an online master's degree program: Perceptions of students and faculty. *Online Journal of Distance Learning Administration, 20*(3). Retrieved 25 February 2022, from https://www.learntechlib.org/p/188480/.

De Souza Fleith, D. (2000). Teacher and student perceptions of creativity in the classroom environment. *Roeper Review*, *22*(3), 148–53.

Kortjass, M. (2015). 'I think I can teach': The preparation of mathematics early childhood education teachers. *Journal of Educational Studies*, *14*(1), 1–19.

Designing an Interview Study

When designing an interview study, you need to first determine whether interviews are the best tool for your study. Once you have chosen interviews as the instrument, you need to think about what kind of interview you need. For kinds of interviews, see Table 1.2.

If you have very limited time with each participant and think that giving them a questionnaire is not an option (possibly because they might not return it or you don't have a way to send a questionnaire

TABLE 1.2 Kinds of Interview

Structured interview	Structured interviews are those which have a strict interview schedule and the researcher does not deviate from the pre-decided set of questions. These are a lot like a questionnaire and are done in market research or street surveys, where giving the participants a questionnaire is not convenient and practical.
Semi-structured interview	Semi-structured interviews are those which have a pre-decided interview schedule but room for follow-up questions and prompts to be used by the researcher depending upon the participants' answers. These are very common in educational research.
Unstructured interview	Unstructured interviews are those where the researcher usually has topics or areas to cover and does not make a list of questions to ask. They are very informal and almost like a conversation. They are commonly used in ethnographic research.

to them), you can go for structured interviews. However, if you think that you need in-depth data and can develop a set of questions to ask but need flexibility to ask follow-up questions, semi-structured interviews are the way to go. If you only have a very broad understanding of the topic and would like to rely on the participants' knowledge to lead the conversation, you might need to go for unstructured interviews.

Once you have decided which interview type you need to use, you can then start working on your interview schedule (see Table 1.1). An interview schedule for qualitative research is prepared based on the researcher's understanding of the topic and context and is guided by the literature. So you will need to read about your topic and see the relevant factors in order to prepare the questions in your protocol. An example interview schedule is presented in Box 1.2.

Box 1.2 Example Interview Schedule

Title: Fiction Teachers' views about impact of novels on students' perceptions

1. Introduction to the project and purpose of the interview are given.
2. What would you say is your teaching methodology? Why do you choose to teach this way? Do you think there are any other possible alternatives?
3. Do you feel fiction has any effects on students' social life?
4. Do you consider students' perception of society (citizenship or identity, rights and duties) when you teach them fiction? Does it come up in the classroom?
5. What do you think about identity, rights and duties in relation to these books? Do you think the fiction they are learning will affect students' perceptions of these social issues?
6. What do you think students think about identity, rights and duties in relation to these novels you teach?
7. Thank you for your time and views.

Activity 1.1 can help you understand the process of designing an interview schedule further.

Activity 1.1 Preparing an Interview Schedule

Imagine you are conducting research on the topic 'British students' perceptions of identity, rights and duties'. Study the literature on the area to find out what factors could affect the students' perceptions. Prepare a list of questions that you would like to ask your participants.

Once you have designed an interview schedule like Activity 1.1, you should then pilot it. This means checking the questions with one or two people to see if they are understandable for the respondents and get you the information that you need. You could also determine how much time one interview takes during the pilot. After the pilot, you have a chance to review and revise your schedule before you can start collecting data from your actual respondents.

Another issue to consider is sampling (see Table 1.1). If you are interested in Pakistani undergraduate students' perceptions regarding cheating in exams, your *population* is all the undergraduate students in Pakistan. Your *sample* would then be the selected participants – let's say twenty participants from a particular university in the country.

Size, access, representativeness and sampling type/strategy need to be considered when selecting a sample. *Size*, that is the number of participants to interview, is limited in interviews as in all qualitative research. Depending on the length of your interview, you can decide on a suitable number of participants. For example, in my PhD study, I did twenty-six semi-structured interviews of roughly an hour each, whereas a colleague of mine did a PhD with six unstructured interviews of two to three hours each.

You need to select participants who you would be able to *access*. If you do not think you can access your participants, you might need to reconsider your research plan. Another factor that you should also think about is how these participants in your sample reflect *and represent* the population that you have selected them from. For example, if your population has 30 per cent men and 70 per cent women, then your sample to some extent should reflect the ratio. However, as this is a qualitative study, we are not aiming for generalizability. You need to finally think about the strategy that you would like to use for sampling. For further reading on sampling strategies, please refer to Cohen, Manion and Morrison (2018).

Ethical Considerations

As in all research dealing with human participants, you have to be very careful about ethical protocols. Common ethical protocol dictates that you prepare a consent form covering all the necessary information about the study and ask your participants to read and sign it. You need to tell your participants about the purpose of the study as well as how the data will be used. Voluntary participation, anonymity and ability to withdraw at any stage should be assured in the consent form. This is especially necessary if you are dealing with any sensitive issues such as identity, bullying and so on or if you are dealing with vulnerable groups such as children or minority groups. You should always take advice from your supervisor regarding ethical issues specific to your dissertation.

Potential Challenges

The potential challenges during an interview study could be recruiting participants, getting detailed answers, dealing with silence and keeping the conversation relevant to your topic. When you decide on the number of participants to approach for your data collection, you should consider that some people may not be available, some may not respond and some may agree and then back out later. So you should always have more accessible participants than you need.

Another issue that you may face is that of getting rich as well as relevant data. Some participants may not speak in as much detail as needed. Some may be silent for longer than expected. For such situations, it is important to have prompts to enable the

pre-prepared prompts

participants to answer questions in detail. For example, I asked my participants, 'How would you describe your identity?' Many participants found it quite a vague and difficult question. So I had prompts prepared to explain the question. For example, 'You can talk about any kind of identity that is important to you like religious, ethnic, linguistic, personal etc.' You should also learn to be comfortable with silence as it might be the first time the participants are thinking about your topic and might need a few moments to collect their thoughts and speak. Explaining the question and rephrasing may also be useful.

As in all data collection, during interviews, you need to collect focussed information related to your topic. Some participants may not stick to the topic and talk about issues irrelevant to your study. In such cases, you need to be vigilant in bringing them back to your topic. Asking the question again, repeating what they say and adding phrases like 'this is very interesting but I am interested in knowing ...' keep the conversation on track without offending the respondents.

Conducting an Interview

You need to be mindful of a number of things while conducting an interview. While setting up an interview, you should consider a place which is suitable for both you and your participant. You should also think about noise levels as you will probably need to record the interview. Try your recording instrument beforehand, and make sure that you have a Plan B, for example, in case your phone runs out of charge. I always record on two different devices simultaneously to avoid the chance of losing the data.

During the data collection stage, we try to keep our own opinions and biases away, so that the interviewee is not affected by our views. To ensure that, you should not ask any leading questions and avoid putting your own opinion across. While introducing your topic, you should think about how much to give away in order to ensure that the interviewee's view is not affected. Always remember that the interview is about the views of the participants; therefore, your job is to encourage and facilitate them to talk rather than giving your own views. Activity 1.2 contains an activity to help you practise.

Activity 1.2 Practising Interviews

Imagine you are researching about undergraduate students' reasons to choose their major. Prepare a list of questions to ask your participants. Think of the factors that could possibly affect a student's choice of major and factor those in while designing your interview protocol. With a friend, practice taking interviews by asking each other the set questions. Think about how flexible you want to be while using your prepared interview questions.

Analysing Interview Data

The first thing involved in the analysis of interview data is transcription (see Table 1.1). You need to write the audio word for word as the participants say it for authenticity. An example transcript is presented in Box 1.3.

Transcription helps you familiarize yourself with the data. Try Activity 1.3 to practise transcription.

Box 1.3 Example Transcript

Interviewer (I): [Introduces topic]. Tell me about yourself, where were you born, how did you grow up?

Respondent (R): Erm ... I was born in Ghotki district, I did my matriculation from there, then I ... I did my intermediate from a government college as well, and then I took admission in University of Sindh. There ... my ... my perception, my standard were totally changed due to literature, due to different company. Now I am in final year in literature class.

I: Throughout your life were there any factors or personalities that made an impact on you?

R: Yes ... There were teachers in higher secondary who had done fresh master's from university, some were from Sindh University, some were from Islamabad. They influenced very much on our ... on our, personalities, we were highly impressed from them and that is why we moved on to University of Sindh. I came to university after that.

I: How about your religious commitments?

R: I believe in religion Islam. Whatever Islam says we have to follow this path.

I: Do you believe in any social or political stance?

R: No.

Once you have transcribed your interviews, you have to organize your data in such a manner that you can report it in your dissertation. In order to organize your data, you need to code your data. Coding is like giving a name or topic to an extract from your data. For an example of coding, please see Table 1.3. It is useful to ask someone else to code a bit of your data as well to check the trustworthiness of your coding.

Activity 1.3 Transcribing an Interview

Transcribe the interview that you collected for Activity 1.2. Remember you need to write the interview word for word. Do not complete the participants' sentences or thoughts, don't change any words or correct any grammatical errors. We want to keep the data authentic.

After you have coded all your data, you can write down your list of codes. List of codes is like a book index – it helps you to find things. The purpose of coding is to be able to categorize similar things across interviews. In order to do that, you need to organize your data according to codes. Once your data is arranged according to codes, you will be able to notice any patterns that emerge in it.

TABLE 1.3 Example Coding

Transcription	Code
I: (Introduces topic). Tell me about yourself, where were you born, how did you grow up? R: Erm … I was born in a village in Ghotki district, I did my matriculation.	Rural background
From there, then I … I did my intermediate from a government college as well, and then I took admission in University of Sindh. There …	Education
My … my perception, my standard were totally changed due to literature, due to different company. Now I am in final year in literature class.	Perceived change
I: Throughout your life were there any factors or personalities that made an impact on you? R: Yes … There were teachers in higher secondary who had done fresh master's from university, some were from Sindh University, some were from Islamabad. They influenced very much on our … on our, personalities, we were highly impressed from them and that is why we moved on to University of Sindh. I came to university after that.	Influence of teachers
I: How about your religious commitments? R: I believe in religion Islam. Whatever Islam says we have to follow this path. I: Do you believe in any social or political stance? R: No.	Religion

For example, if you were doing a study about 'challenges teachers face while teaching online', you might have coded data under codes such as 'classroom management' and 'group activities'. Once you have the data under these two codes, you might be able to identify that novice teachers face challenges in classroom management while more experienced teachers manage online classes through group activities. This could be one of the themes or arguments that you discuss in your findings. So the coding process helps draw out common themes across interviews. These themes are discussed with the help of data extracts in your dissertation. There are many different ways to analyse qualitative data; the one discussed here is _Thematic Analysis_. Even though other types of analyses you may read about are slightly different, they do make use of transcription and coding of data as some of the key features. You can practise coding in Activity 1.4.

Activity 1.4 Coding

Code the transcript given below. Use the codes below:

– Context   – Motivation   – Challenges   – Planning

Q. How long have you been teaching English for?

A. It's been almost six years now.

Q. Why did you decide to become a teacher?

A. After I did my master's, I felt like teaching was the only job I could take up.

Q. Do you still feel that way?

A. Yes, the thing that I like most about my profession is sharing knowledge.

Q. How much workload do you have?

A. I have three to four classes every day of one-hour each, five days a week.

Q. How much time does your planning take?

A. It hardly takes me half an hour to prepare for each class.

When Not to Use Interviews

Interviews are not a suitable instrument when you are looking for quick and short answers (see Chapter 3). When you are interested in actions rather than opinions and beliefs, interviews are not an appropriate tool (see Chapter 4). Interviews are also not used in studies that seek to get generalizable results. For example, if you wish to determine what the views of Spanish undergraduate students are regarding online teaching and learning, you will need to do a quantitative study with a large number of participants, rather than interviews. Interview data is good for in-depth study and not generalizability.

Reference

Cohen, L., Manion, L., & Morrison, K. (2018). *Research methods in education* (Eighth edition). London: Routledge.

CHAPTER TWO
Focus Groups
Elizabeth Bailey

What Can This Method Tell Me?

Focus groups (sometimes called a *group interview* or a *focus group interview*) allow us insight into a group of people's views, perceptions, attitudes or opinions on a particular topic. Both the *focus* and the *group* are important when it comes to this method of collecting data. That is, there will usually be something specific you want to know about and a specific group of people you want to hear from.

Holding a group discussion allows us to look at agreement and disagreement within a group. It can prompt people to discuss things they may not have otherwise thought of discussing. It also allows the researcher to analyse the group interaction itself, not just individuals' thoughts. So, with a focus group, we can easily see where any points of contention are on a particular topic as the group debates these together. Similarly, we can see where the group agrees, and they may come to some kind of consensus on the topic at hand. This is why focus groups are often used in market research. In this case, businesses can see where there might be problems with a product, whether the group likes the name, or the packaging, and so on.

When Might I Use It?

You are likely to use a focus group (or a series of focus groups) when you want to know about a specific group of people's thoughts on a particular topic and, importantly, you want to look at the data that comes from them discussing these topics *together*.

Let's imagine you are looking at the topic of school uniforms, for example. From just thinking about the people you know personally, you can probably already think of different opinions that might be held about this topic. For example, we might discuss (i) whether school uniforms should be worn or not, (ii) what items should be included in uniforms or (iii) whether school uniforms restrict young people's opportunities to express themselves or, in fact, prevent social exclusion and bullying. We can already see that some of these issues are complex, and when we want to better understand this complexity, or to find a solution to a problem, even, asking a group of people can allow us to more efficiently gain the insight we need.

There are three fundamental things to think about when planning a focus group to ensure it runs smoothly and allows you to collect the data you're looking for.

1. The number of people taking part: Focus groups usually involve between four and twelve people. You need enough people to keep the discussion flowing, yet not so many that the conversation becomes unmanageable and people are left out. As we'll see, group dynamics play a big part in focus groups.

2. The length of time the discussion lasts: While the discussion needs to last long enough to ensure everyone has the chance to speak, it is important that they don't take too long, and your participants remain engaged and happy to be there. Usually, around one to two hours is about right. Remember, you'll need to transcribe and analyse all the data, too. Long focus groups can make this process unmanageable, depending on the time you have.

3. The setting: You need your participants to feel willing and safe to speak their mind. This is even more important with more contentious or sensitive topics and with young or vulnerable participants. In such cases, it is also

worth considering whether a group environment is the best fit. <u>While it may help people to open up and to feel less vulnerable than in a one-on-one discussion with a researcher, it can also add extra pressure.</u> This is important from an ethical point of view as it is our duty to keep our participants safe. Participants' level of comfort also affects our data and the likelihood of them speaking freely and openly (which is what we want). This is also why selecting your group carefully is important.

Let's continue to think about the topic of school uniforms. Imagine you conduct one focus group with head teachers and one with students. Look at the extracts in Box 2.1 to see what the data you collect might look like when it's written out from the audio recording (transcribed).

Box 2.1 Two Sample Extracts from Focus Group Transcripts for the School Uniform Project

Head Teacher Focus Group

Head teacher 1: We have a uniform policy because we see it as our duty to prepare students for the real world in which they will be expected to dress smartly.

Head teacher 2: That's right. It is a key responsibility of schools to equip students with the skills and experience they need for the working world.

Head teacher 3: It's not about popularity. It's about responsibility. We are expected to have a uniform policy. Parents expect it. The governors expect it.

Student Focus Group

Student 1: I want to be able to choose my own clothes because I want to be able to dress how I like.

> Student 2: Yes, why can't we have that freedom? I think uniforms are outdated to be honest.
> Student 1: Yeah, it's not like that many jobs need you to wear smart clothes anyway, is it?
> Student 3: Yeah, my Mum works from home and she doesn't wear a suit or anything like that.
> Student 4: And in your job, you can choose whether you wear a blazer in summer or not, or have your top button done up or not.

The discussion in both these extracts provides you with different data on the same topic. Now, imagine how these data might be different had we conducted a focus group with head teachers and students in the same group. Do you think everyone would have said the same thing? What about if the group were all strangers to one another? This is why, often, but not always, focus groups are conducted with pre-existing groups of people (e.g. classmates or colleagues). It helps to maximize the benefits of the method when everyone is relaxed and speaks freely.

Ultimately, the group dynamics affect the data you collect and therefore affect the results of your project. That is why designing them carefully really matters. The most important thing to keep in mind is why you're asking what you're asking, and why you're asking those people in particular. Your topic, your group of participants and your research questions should all align. For example, if you're interested in the rationale behind school uniform policy, a group of head teachers are likely to be who you ask. If you're interested in how the school uniform affects students' perceptions of difference, it's likely that students would be your focus.

One thing that can happen in any focus group is that the conversation ends before you would like it to. This is why it is important to consider the structure of your discussion beforehand. Will you have a list of questions, or points, that you ensure are covered, for example? This is known as a discussion guide.

Focus groups allow you to take what's called a *structured* or *unstructured* approach, just like interviews (see Chapter 1). That is, you can have a very clear discussion guide (structured), where you retain a lot of control over the direction of the dialogue. This may involve providing questions, quotes, pictures or a short task, even. Alternatively, you can allow your participants more freedom to respond to the topic and have very few open prompts, or no prompts at all (unstructured). There's no right or wrong, it's just important to think about whether you need the discussion to be tightly focused in order to answer your research question(s). Generally speaking, the more specific your research questions are, the more you need to keep the group tightly focused on the topic.

Consider the prompts in Box 2.2. They illustrate the importance of really thinking about how you want to keep the discussion flowing.

Box 2.2 A List of Example Questions and Prompts That Might Be Used in a Focus Group

- Does anyone have any further comments on that?
- Now let's look at Picture 3. Who would like to start us off thinking about this one?
- Do you agree or disagree with the quote on the board?
- Has anyone else experienced that feeling?
- Could you tell me more about that?
- Let's move on to the next discussion item on your list.
- Now we've talked about the advantages, can anyone tell me about the disadvantages?

Take a few moments to imagine how the discussion might play out after each of these prompts. For some, it is easier to imagine what comes next than for others because these offer more control over the direction of the discussion.

Finally, we need to think about your role as the researcher in the focus group. As the researcher, you will need to make sure everyone has the information they need and that they are comfortable and happy to participate. This is part of conducting an ethical study. It is likely that you will also take on the role of *moderator* in your focus group(s), although not all focus groups have a moderator.

If you're also moderating, and it is a more structured focus group, you'll need to ensure that the discussion guide is followed and you use the prompts you need to (should you need to). This can take practice, and it is a really important role. There are lots of factors to consider as part of this role, and things may happen that you had not planned for. To start you thinking, look at the questions in Box 2.3 and see if you can think about how you would answer them. You may not need to deal with some of these issues, but it is good practice to think about how you *would*. You could also try practising being a moderator with a group of friends before you start your project.

Box 2.3 A List of Questions to Consider When You're Undertaking the Moderator Role

1. When will you use prompts? How often?
2. How will you pace the discussion so that you cover everything you need to?
3. How will you deal with someone (or several people) who are dominating the conversation?
4. How will you ensure everyone has the chance to speak?
5. How will you deal with someone who begins to look uncomfortable, or tells you they wish to leave?

Terminology

Table 2.1 includes some of the key terms you will come across. Some of these terms have already been used and the others will be used when we talk about designing a focus group and analysing the data we get, later. Let's check your understanding of each before we move on.

Design of a Dissertation Project with This Method/Tool

Remember, focus groups are best suited to looking at people's thoughts on a particular topic. When it comes to education, there are so many things that people have different opinions on. Any area

TABLE 2.1 Focus Group Vocabulary

Discussion guide	Sometimes also called a *topic guide*, this is a list of questions (although these may be statements or pictures, rather than questions) that are used to structure the focus group. A completely unstructured focus group would not have a discussion guide, however.
Prompts	These are short phrases or questions, often related to the questions in your discussion guide, that help to keep the conversation flowing. When and if they are used is down to individual researchers/moderators (as shown in Box 2.3).
Moderator	This is the person running the group. Often, but not always, a focus group will have a person in this role to ensure the discussion flows and the discussion guide is followed (where there is one).
Purposive recruitment	Purposive recruitment, or sampling, is where we actively select the participants we will include in the study. Unlike in some research, they are not selected at random but are chosen for a specific reason. It makes sense that we recruit in this way for focus groups as we are interested in a specific group of people, and usually, we recruit people we have access to and who may know each other already (e.g. all newly qualified teachers in a given school). It's important to remember that this means we cannot generalize our findings to the whole population (e.g. all newly qualified teachers).
Transcript	Once the focus group has been recorded, everything that has been said will need to be written down ready to be analysed. This process is called transcribing, and the document is called a transcript.

where there is some level of choice, or potential for change, works well, as do studies where the main purpose is to hear from one particular group. We then use purposive recruitment to put together a focus group with people who represent that group. For example,

- you might want to hear from newly qualified teachers about their attitudes towards the support they receive during their first year of teaching;

- you might want to hear from parents of children who recently went to secondary school on what they thought was the best way to support this transition; or

- you might want to hear from teenage girls on their perceptions of the pressures of social media whilst at school.

All of these examples look to gain collective insight into a specific area. They don't aim to *measure* attitudes, like a questionnaire may aim to. They don't look to explore *individual* stories and experiences, like an interview may look to. Chapters 1 and 3 can tell you more about these two methods.

When deciding whether a focus group is right for your project, you can think about the key suitability criteria in Box 2.4, where your answer to each should be yes.

Box 2.4 Key Suitability Criteria for a Focus Group

- Do I have a specific group of people I need to hear from?
- Do I have a clear topic?
- Is it ok if I don't know who is speaking the whole time?
- Am I more interested in the group, rather than the individual?
- Can I access this group to hold a focus group?
- Can I expect this group to discuss this topic together?

It is also worth remembering that focus groups often fit well with other methods as a means of gaining more data on a topic in an efficient way. They can complement questionnaires well, for example.

The final aspect of the design of your focus group you want to consider is the potential for this to be held online. You could use a group video chat, or even a group chat box, to conduct a focus group with people anywhere in the world. This allows you access to people you may not usually be able to meet if you had to physically meet in person. It, therefore, broadens what you could look at, as well as with whom you can carry out your research. Plus, it reduces the burden on your participants as they don't have to travel. They may also feel more comfortable in their own home, without having to physically interact with the other group members.

Online focus groups may also cause people to feel less comfortable, less engaged and less willing to share their thoughts, however, because they may be less comfortable with the online experience. You can also only involve people who can use the software you need them to and who are happy and able to use the technology. You need to weigh up the pros and cons for your study and the people you'd like to involve. There's also lots to think about in terms of ethics: how you will keep the discussion private and secure or how you will ensure no one's personal data is shared (e.g. their email address) as well as decisions such as whether you will use video, or audio, and which of these you will record, for example. These are all things you can seek advice on as part of the research journey.

Analysis

Focus groups are a method used in qualitative research. As such, there is no one set way to analyse them. You'll need to think carefully about the analysis process you're going to undertake and keep a careful record of it. In educational research, data from focus groups are usually analysed using thematic analysis; so, here, I'm going to demonstrate to you what this might look like.

Let's go back to the example of a focus group on the topic of school uniform. Let's say that you hold a focus group with seven students in their first year of secondary school and ask them about how they have found wearing their new uniform. When reading carefully through the data, you will find times when the group repeat ideas: for example, the idea that their uniform helped them to settle into the school, it helped them to feel part of the community and it helped them to identify as a school member. Through your analysis, you may then decide that all of these belong to the same theme that you call *integrating in the school*.

This is very much the same process as you would undertake when conducting thematic analysis on any data (e.g. from an interview). The key thing to remember with a focus group is that you have multiple people speaking. It's unlikely you'll be able to look at individuals' contributions because you will have less data from one person compared with an interview. You may also not be able to distinguish who is speaking all the time, depending on how fast paced and overlapping the speech was. That's why it's best to think of the data as a group's contribution to the project, rather than many individuals all at once. Every focus group is different, however, and you'll need to think about the best way to analyse yours. Plus, it is normal for your data analysis plan to evolve as you go.

If you'd like to see focus groups being used in educational research, take some time to look at the studies in Box 2.5.

Box 2.5 Studies in the Field of Education Using Focus Groups as a Method

- Hajar, A. (2020). The association between private tutoring and access to grammar schools: Voices of Year 6 pupils and teachers in south-east England. *British Educational Research Journal, 46*(3), 459–79.
- Beserra, V., Nussbaum, M., Navarrete, M., & Alvares, D. (2021). Teaching through dance: An opportunity to introduce physically active academic lessons. *Teaching and Teacher Education, 104*(10345), 1–13.
- Rosen, L. H., Scott, S. R., & DeOrnellas, K. (2017). Teachers' perceptions of bullying: A focus group approach. *Journal of School Violence, 16*(1), 119–39.

What This Method Is Not Suitable for?

We've already touched briefly on what a focus group *can't* do throughout this chapter, but let's remind ourselves of the type of projects, or research questions, that focus groups might not be the best fit for.

So, first things first, a focus group research project needs to be suitable for a group of people and it needs to be suitable for looking at one specific issue (or a number of related issues). So, if it is an individual you're interested in, if it is detailed, personal stories and experiences, you should consider using interviews instead. Equally, if you are unsure of what you want to look at, individual interviews can offer more flexibility to pursue specific avenues when they arise. You have more control. In a focus group, your participants have a lot of control over the conversation and, subsequently, the data that you have to analyse.

Even if you have a specific topic and a specific group of people you could use for a focus group, it is sometimes not the right route. Here's where the group element really matters again. Ask yourself the following: Would you be happy discussing every topic in a group? With your peers? With strangers? With a researcher? If you think your topic might cause people distress in a group situation, or it involves them sharing personal stories, consider whether they would feel more comfortable in a one-on-one interview.

Finally, from a more practical point of view, it is important to think about your own time and capacity to conduct a focus group. You will need to arrange the discussion, coordinate participants' schedules and (potentially) prepare to moderate the discussion. A lot of organization goes into focus groups, and you only really have one chance to get it right. It's a method that has a lot of potential, but only if it's right for you and your participants.

Timing - Ensuring all can participate at same time.
(Take them out of a workshop?)

CHAPTER THREE

Questionnaires

Abigail Parrish

What Can They Tell Me?

Questionnaires are useful when you want to find out something that is in someone's head. This might be their views on something, or their perceptions or experiences of something. If your participants are going to be able to answer the questions you ask them, particularly if they can do this by giving short answers, ticking boxes or choosing from options, then questionnaires might be a good method to use.

When Might I Use Them?

Imagine that you wanted to answer the broad question, 'What is marking like in schools?' There are several things you might want to know here, many of which can be addressed with a questionnaire. For example,

- You want to know teachers' views on marking: do they enjoy it?
- You want to know how often they do it.
- You want to know whether their school has a strict policy on how marking is carried out.

You could find these things out with a questionnaire to teachers because (i) they know the answers and (ii) the answers you need are not particularly detailed. Box 3.1 gives an example of a question you could use.

Box 3.1 A Sample Extract from a Questionnaire Focused on Marking

How do you feel about marking?	
I enjoy it very much	☐
I quite enjoy it	☐
I don't enjoy it	☐
I hate it	☐

You can see from Box 3.1 that it is possible to use a questionnaire to get right to the core of what you want to know if you ask the right people the right questions.

But maybe what you actually want to know is whether students feel that they get useful feedback. Teachers can't tell you this – they can tell you whether the students tell *them* that they get useful feedback, but this is now quite far from the original source of the opinion. If you did a questionnaire with students themselves (see Box 3.2), you could get at this information much more directly. It is important to make sure you ask the right people and can get access to the right people.

Box 3.2 A Sample Extract from a Questionnaire Focused on Feedback

How do you feel about the feedback you get from your teacher?	
I don't get any feedback	☐
It's sometimes useful	☐
It's often useful	☐
It's always useful	☐

Now imagine that you wanted to find out what the school's marking policy was. You could ask teachers, but the responses you would get would be *their interpretation* of the marking policy. The same would happen if you asked students. Teachers' – or students' – interpretations of the policy are not the same as what the policy is, and so this would not be a sensible way of going about this.

The other problem here is that this is not a very good question for a questionnaire – you couldn't answer this with tick boxes. You would have to ask for what are called 'open text comments' – for people to write a response in their own words. Some people would write very short answers: for example, 'mark books once a week; use highlighters'. Others would give much more detail. But what would be the value in collecting answers to this question from each participant? It would be much more efficient, and informative, to get a copy of the marking policy and analyse it yourself (see Chapter 5).

There is a way that questionnaires might help you with this question, though. Perhaps you have studied the marking policies in a range of schools and you are now putting out a questionnaire about marking online, so you don't know which schools teachers come from. Based on what you know about marking policies, you might design some questions to find out what kind of policy they are working with before you go on to ask other questions.

This approach would allow you to identify what general kind of marking policy respondents were working to. However, you would still need to consider how useful this was. For example, do you need to know what colour pens are used? Should you specify within the question, as in Box 3.3? What if they use green instead of purple for self-marking? Is the colour itself relevant to your project? More importantly, how would you expect a participant to answer if you haven't given them an option that accurately describes what is done in their school? Perhaps your question should be 'a particular colour for self-marking' – and if the colour were relevant, you could add a box to allow them to either enter the colour or choose from a list.

Box 3.3 A Sample Extract from a Questionnaire Focused on Marking Policy

What are the features of your school's marking policy? Tick all that apply.	
Purple pens for self-marking	☐
Purple pens for peer marking	☐
Red pens for teacher marking	☐
Highlighters	☐
Dynamic marking	☐
Marking codes	☐
Marking every lesson	☐
Marking once a term	☐
No teacher marking in books	☐

I hope this section has shown you that questionnaires can be useful in a lot of projects, but that you need to think carefully about whether they are useful in *your* project and whether you are asking the right people the right questions. Box 3.6 gives you an example of a real-life project using a questionnaire.

Terminology

Before we move on to look at designing, distributing and analysing questionnaires, we need to learn some of the technical terms, shown in Table 3.1. Like many things, research has its own vocabulary, and understanding this helps you to understand research methods textbooks and sound convincing when you discuss your work with your supervisor.

TABLE 3.1 Questionnaire Vocabulary

Term	Meaning
Item	A particular 'question' on your questionnaire. Sometimes this is not actually a question – it might be a statement that you ask participants to agree or disagree with.
Scale	A set of questionnaire items which are designed to measure something in particular – for example, motivation.
Instrument	The questionnaire itself.
Participants/respondents	The people who take part in your questionnaire.

Questionnaire Design

Potential Problems

We have started to see above that designing a questionnaire requires a lot of thought. It can be easy to imagine that you can just jot down a list of questions and use them, but you need to be careful. Can your questions be answered? How many things are you asking your participants to think about in each one? Do they make grammatical sense?

Activity 3.1 Potential Problems

Have another look at Boxes 3.2 and 3.3. Can you see any potential problems with the example questionnaire items?

Box 3.4 considers some potential problems with the questionnaires from Boxes 3.2 and 3.3.

Box 3.4 Potential Problems with Questionnaire Items

Sample item	Potential problem
What are the features of your school's marking policy? Tick all that apply	What if the participant works in a college? Is this a problem? What if they don't have a whole-school policy?
Purple pens for peer marking ☐	'At my school, we use green pens for peer marking.' Should this respondent tick the box? What do you really want to know: the colour of the pen, the presence of peer marking or the use of a specific colour pen for peer marking, regardless of colour? Each of those would potentially require a slightly different question.
Dynamic marking ☐	What if the respondent hasn't heard this term – or what if they use dynamic marking but call it something different?
Marking once a term ☐	Maybe the policy says 'once every six lessons'. This could be once a term for some subjects, but once a week for others. But maybe it says once every five lessons, or four … What should your question look like? This will need careful thinking about.
How do you feel about the feedback you get from your teacher?	Which teacher?

Sample item		Potential problem
It's sometimes useful	☐	What do you think the students understand by 'useful'? Do you need to be more specific?
It's often very useful	☐	'Often useful' and 'very useful' are two different things. It might be often quite useful, or sometimes very useful. How are you going to unpick this? Do you need to find out about both? Perhaps you need separate questions.
Indicate how much you agree with the following statements: My teacher gives me useful feedback. Do you like school? ☐		Here, you would give tick boxes to indicate agreement. But how do you agree with a question like 'Do you like school?' You can agree with a statement like 'I like school'. But 'Do you like school?' requires a different type of response, probably yes/no.

Response Options

There are a large variety of question types that you can use in your questionnaire. Some of the most common are multiple choice and Likert scale questions. You are no doubt familiar with multiple choice questions, where respondents can choose from one of a range of options. There might be only two choices (this is also known as a binary response question; often it would be a choice between 'yes' or 'no'), or there might be a longer list. Participants may be able to choose one or more than one option. There may be an 'other' option, which may ask the participants to specify.

Likert scales are also very common, and you will no doubt have come across them, even if you don't know the name. In a Likert scale question, there is a statement or question followed by a list of items and a scale to tick, as shown in Box 3.5.

Box 3.5 A Sample Likert Scale Question

Please indicate how much you agree with the following statements:

	Strongly agree	Agree	Disagree	Strongly disagree
My teacher gives useful feedback	□	□	□	□
My teacher gives regular feedback	□	□	□	□
My teacher talks me through the feedback he or she has given	□	□	□	□

Likert scales can have almost any number of points, although four or five is probably most common. By having four, or another even number, as above, participants are forced to have an opinion. If you have an odd number, you can add a neutral option, for example 'neither agree nor disagree'.

Alternatively, you could use one of your options for 'don't know' or 'not applicable'. This is a decision you will have to make for your own questionnaire, and it is important to think not only about how you will analyse your results, but also about what you can expect of your participants. Can you expect them all to have an opinion or be able to give an answer? If so, perhaps you don't need a neutral response option.

Administering Your Questionnaire

One important decision you will make is whether to put your questionnaire online or do it on paper. There are many online questionnaires or survey tools which you can use, and your university may well subscribe to one which would be a good option.

Online questionnaires have many advantages. Some of the design work is done by the online tool, so you don't have to think about layout. You can change the settings, so that certain questions only appear if participants give particular answers (e.g. if you ask, 'Has your book been marked this term?' and the answer is 'no', then there is no point asking questions about how useful the feedback was). You can force participants to give an answer before they move on to the next question. You do not have to worry about handwriting or rogue ticks, and you will have your results in one place ready to analyse. You can access participants over a wider geographical area and they can complete the questionnaire in their own time.

However, you may prefer to use paper questionnaires. Perhaps your participants don't have computer or internet access, or perhaps you think they are too young (or too old!) to use the technology. The problem here is that you will have to decipher handwriting, work out where ticks were intended to be (which can be surprisingly difficult sometimes) and contend with surveys which are only half completed, where participants chose not to answer every question. You will also have to enter the results into the computer for analysis and manage the photocopying, and potentially postage, costs as well as consider the environmental impact.

Gaining access to participants may also be a problem – people are very busy and your questionnaire is unlikely to be top of their list of priorities. If you can give a good indication of how long it will take, this will help, but you will still likely have to send out several reminders. You may gain access via specific schools, which can help to get a large number of student participants, as each class will probably have around 30 students so one teacher can help you get a lot of data. You will need to think about how much time your questionnaire will take and whether it is ethical for students to miss lesson time to complete it.

You might also gain access to participants through organizations (such as subject associations) or groups (e.g. on social media). You will have less control over who completes your questionnaire this way, so you need to consider whether that is important or not.

One big question when it comes to questionnaires is 'How many responses do I need?' The answer to this is generally 'as many as possible', especially if you are planning to do statistical analyses, but response rates are hard to predict and can be influenced by a range of factors, including who your participants are (head teachers or vice chancellors are likely to be busier than students, and there are substantially fewer of them), what you are asking about (sensitive topics or topics not many people know about will be harder to recruit for) and when you ask (exam season is likely to be a time when people are busy with other things, for example). Nevertheless, you should aim for as good a response rate as possible, which may mean sending out reminders. Make sure you plan for this in advance so you can make them as effective as possible.

Analysis

Analysing your questionnaire can be done in different ways. You may wish to do some statistical analysis – if you do, you will need a suitable statistics program and some know-how. You will also need quite a lot of responses – one class is probably not enough. If you are considering this, get hold of a good statistics textbook to read more about it. If you can, statistical tests that allow you to compare responses between groups or look for correlations will make your project much stronger, but make sure you allow plenty of time to learn how to do this.

You may prefer to do simpler analyses, like calculating percentages and counting up numbers of responses in particular categories. You can do this on Excel, and for many projects, this will be enough. You may generate charts to show your data visually or tables to present it succinctly. It is important that you do this in ways that make your data clear. For example, you will need to think about the scales used in charts. You should never try to compare data on one chart where the axis goes up to 80 per cent with one where it goes up to 100 per cent – what you see will be misleading. Don't rely on what Excel produces for you – you may have to change things to get it looking how you want. It is easy to find short tutorials for Excel online.

It is not the case that more is more when it comes to presenting data. Think about the most efficient, and clearest, way that you can show your findings. For example, do you need separate charts, or can you include data from multiple questions on one? Keep in mind that what you are trying to do is make the data that you have collected easy to understand for your audience. How you do that will depend on a variety of things, but you need to do the hard work and make it simple for the reader to understand what you have found and how you have come to your conclusions.

What Questionnaires Are Not Suitable for?

If your participants cannot reasonably be expected to know the answer to your questions, questionnaires will not help you. This may be because you are using the wrong participants or the wrong method. For example, if you wanted to know what head teachers thought of marking in their schools, asking the teachers or students would not give you very useful answers – it would be guesswork and supposition at best. But, if you asked head teachers themselves, then a questionnaire might work. However, if you wanted to know how often teachers gave verbal feedback in a lesson, although you could use a questionnaire, you would be better off using observations (see Chapter 4), so that you could see this in action. A questionnaire would give you teachers' impressions of how often they gave feedback as they looked back over the lesson, which may or may not be accurate.

Questionnaires give you an overview and show trends. They give you the 'what', and often the 'how', but rarely the 'why'. This may mean that you need to mix two methods – a quantitative method, like questionnaires, and a qualitative method, like interviews.

Box 3.6 Questionnaires in Use

Questionnaires are very commonly used in academic research, and many journal articles report studies which use them. One example is the paper below, which included something called the Self-Regulation Questionnaire (Academic), (available at https://selfdeterminationtheory.org/self-regulation-questionnaires/). A questionnaire was used because we wanted to understand students' motivation to do their work in their modern foreign languages lessons, which meant asking them questions; and we wanted to be able to compare our findings with other studies of motivation, which meant using a method that was already established in the literature. Questionnaires were the best method because we could gather a lot of data quickly to allow us to understand trends.

Parrish, A., & Ursula Lanvers, U. (2019). Student motivation, school policy choices and modern language study in England. *The Language Learning Journal, 47*(3), 281–98. doi: 10.1080/09571736.2018.1508305.

CHAPTER FOUR

Observations

Géraldine Bengsch

What Can They Tell Me?

Observations can help you gain new insights into a topic that you are already familiar with by looking at it through a different lens. They can provide you with rich descriptions of your participants' lived experiences. Observations can be really useful at highlighting differences between what people say they do (e.g. reported behaviour in interviews or questionnaires) and what they actually do. An observation does not rely on your participants' memory or willingness to recall their actions. Observations, live or recorded, are an example of real-time research; that is, the researcher is able to collect data at the same time as the phenomenon being researched takes place. It involves investigation of more than what people are saying and doing. You can also generate insights into culture, social norms and social practices.

When Might I Use Them?

Consider observations when you want to experience a phenomenon through the viewpoint of your participants. Observations are also useful when you want to explore and describe a phenomenon that has not been described before. They can help you to find naturally emerging patterns in behaviour, when you

- want direct information;
- are trying to understand an ongoing behaviour process, unfolding situation or event;
- are in a situation with physical evidence, products or outcomes that can be readily seen; and
- think that written or other data collection methods seem inappropriate.

You could find these things out with an observation of teachers in the classroom because (i) that is where the phenomenon you are interested in occurs and (ii) the environment will allow you to gather rich and detailed data on your participants. Box 4.3 gives a real-life example of research using observations, and the activity in Box 4.1 gives you a practice observation that you can try right now.

Box 4.1 Practising Observations: Points of View

Try these activities to help you hone your observation skills.

1. Look at the room you are currently sitting in and take five minutes to write down detailed notes about it.
2. Move to a different side of the room and repeat the activity.

Reflection: How did you approach the activity? How are the descriptions different depending on the point of view? What was your stance as a researcher as you completed the exercise? How has your prior knowledge of the room shaped how you see the room?

As you tried the activity above, you will probably have noted that the data you collect is not independent of you, the researcher. This is important because something as simple as moving to a different part of the classroom may affect what you are able to observe. You are likely to have to make accommodations during your fieldwork to ensure that your presence does not disturb your participants. This might mean that you will take your notes from the back of the class or some other not so great position. Researching real life is often far from ideal; consider what this might mean for the notes you can and cannot take.

Observations allow you to study social life as it occurs and offer you an opportunity to highlight practices in everyday life that we usually take for granted and may believe we fully understand. Imagine that you are interested in feedback practices during group work. You likely have an idea of what this entails. You could ask teachers about their practices and ask students about how they perceive them using interviews (see Chapter 1). Observing teachers will not give you such insights into the values that inform their teaching. However, interviews will not give you information on the dynamics that are negotiated on a day-to-day basis in the classroom regarding feedback during group work. If that is what you are interested in, observation gives you a way of seeing familiar things through a different lens and exploring them in depth.

Observations can provide useful data, but you need to consider what you are trying to find out. If you want to ask a lot of people a similar set of questions quickly, you might want to consider using questionnaires (see Chapter 3). If you are interested in what individuals think about a situation, you might want to consider in-depth interviews or focus groups (see Chapter 2). Choose a method that helps you answer *your* question, not one you like the sound of; observations appear deceptively easy. However, keep in mind that they will generate a large amount of highly unstructured data that you need to make sense of, which takes practice, time and patience.

Terminology

Before we move on to look at doing and analysing observations, we need to learn some of the technical terms, which are shown in Table 4.1.

TABLE 4.1 Observation Vocabulary

Term	Meaning
Field work	The 'field' refers to the place where you make your observation. This can be a classroom or other location
Coding	Assigning meaning to data that you collected
Data	The notes that you made
Themes	The main ideas you extract from all of your data
Researcher identity	What you do and how you do it is informed by yourselves and your morals, politics, faith, lifestyle, childhood, values and so on. This is your researcher identity.
Power	Power imbalances in a research project can occur when you are working with children or marginalized groups

Design of an Observation Study

Observations form part of the qualitative research paradigm. This means that it is common to start with a general research area and aim and refine the actual questions over the course of the research project. Often, you start out with a 'hunch' that social practices are different than what they are commonly seen as without knowing exactly how so. You might be interested in how technology is used in a secondary school classroom. This topic may be refined to looking into effective or ineffective use of technology in the language learning classroom and further into how teachers use technology to increase participation of less-engaged students. It is common for research questions to evolve once you have begun gathering your data. You might find that making observations will highlight aspects of practice that you had not previously considered, which can change the direction of your research.

Ethical Considerations

Observations give you access to the inner workings of an organization, such as a school, a classroom, a group of students and their teacher. As such, your presence may affect how your participants behave because they know that they are being observed. It might be tempting to do your observations covertly to avoid this. However, this kind of 'eavesdropping' is largely unacceptable in educational social science research. Your participants should be aware of situations in which they are being observed, so that they can consent to them, and potential harm is minimized. Keeping yourself and your participants safe is highly important, especially when working with children. Not everything you can observe should be observed. Consider the impact that your observations may have with the following activity:

Activity 4.1 Practising Observations: Changing Perspective

1. Imagine you occupy a role other than student at your university (e.g. cleaner, administrator, lecturer).
2. Describe how the university looks, how it works, from your new viewpoint.
3. How would this perspective change what is important to you on a day-to-day basis?
4. How would the interpretation of the same space change the story that is told?

Observations in academic research aim to provide a neutral perspective on social practices. However, we have seen that the researcher plays a significant role in shaping their project and its focus. The way you phrase your research problem will inform what you will pay attention to in your observations. Consider what it is that you are interested in within the given context: Is it the role that teachers play? Students? The interplay between them? These notions will also affect how and where you conduct your observations as well as how much data you will need to collect for your project.

Potential Problems

Observations do not just rely on access to a field to conduct your research in. You also need to consider what kind of role you will be occupying in the community. Ask yourself what a legitimate role would be for you in that environment and allow time for this to develop before you begin your observation. There are a number of aspects to consider, which are discussed below.

Power

Consider the individuals you will be observing. If you are working with children or marginalized groups, you need to consider the power structures that exist and your role within them. How can you avoid being associated with threatening power structures?

Dress

The way you dress marks you either as part of a group or as an outsider. Before you begin your observations in the field, think about the role that you will take and what that means for the way you dress. You may find that certain organizations will request that you present yourself in a certain way. This may be the case in organizations in which uniforms may be the norm. However, even if you try to blend in with students, it is likely that the way you present yourself is more like the teacher, rather than the uniform the students wear. This in turn will affect the way you are seen, as you are clearly not one of the students. Dress can affect how participants view existing power structures.

Language

The language you use to describe your research within your chosen methodology and methods is filled with technical jargon. This is appropriate to converse with your peers and write concisely in your dissertation. However, the way you talk to your participants about and during your observation needs to match their lived reality. You effectively aim to 'translate' your research so that it makes sense to your participants. Remember that you chose the observational site because the individuals there are experts in the phenomenon you are interested in. Make sure that you treat them as such. They may not know the technical vocabulary that you are required to use in your report, but converting the information you gather into academic writing is your job, not your participants'. The way you use language will make it easier or harder to build rapport with your participants. How you talk about your project can make people become self-conscious.

Interaction on Site

The way you interact – or not – with other participants on site will depend on various factors. Observations are usually tied to negotiations with the organizations they occur in. Thus, you may be given access to a school based on certain conditions. A condition could be to not interact with students; however, it could also be that you are expected to help in the classroom. When designing your research project, you need to be clear what an ideal observation will look like and the type of compromises you can make to still be able to answer your research questions. Teachers and students are often used to outsiders coming into the classroom to observe a lesson – for example, by student teachers or for quality evaluations. You may be asked to model these expected behaviours. If you need a particular type of interaction during your observational period to address your research question, make sure that you address this when negotiating access.

Overall, you can expect to be uncomfortable, a bit scared or even mistrusted during your observation. Do not take it personally: paranoia is normal in the field!

Conducting Observations

Observations are commonly conducted in situ: that is, the researcher is present in the same environment as the participants. However, technology can be used for video-based observations through conferencing software, such as Zoom; in some cases, you may want to consider asynchronous observational options and work with videotaped data. Entering an organization creates a significant amount of work for the individuals affected. The specific class you may be interested in is embedded into a wider bureaucratic network which needs to consent to your presence in their environment. This often makes access to the field difficult. Consider what you can offer the school to help minimize the impact your presence has. You may want to avoid particularly busy periods during the year to increase your chances of being allowed into the classroom. It is difficult to generalize how many individual observations you may need for your project or how many different teachers you may want to observe. Each observational instance will yield vast amounts of data, so keep your time constraints for your project in mind. Again, you may be more successful in gaining access to a school if you can concentrate your presence in the class to a minimal amount necessary for your project specifics. If you are interested in how students' engagement with their teachers changes throughout the year, you will need multiple visits to the same cohort. However, if you are interested in how various teachers introduce a new subject, you may only need to observe each class once.

Taking Good Field Notes

Your notes do not have to be pretty. If you are the sole researcher, they also do not have to make sense to anyone but you – but they do certainly need to make sense to you. You can take notes during the observation, or after the event, if you think that taking notes would be too obtrusive. They are invaluable to recall sufficient details about the interaction that you are observing. Make sure that your notes are consistent, to provide you with comparable data. Begin each entry with the date, time, place and data collection event. If you are taking notes in the field, you are likely to take them with pen and paper. To increase efficiency, take notes strategically and consider developing your own shorthand to quickly note down events. Make sure to cover a range of observations and make time to expand your notes as soon as possible after the initial observation, while your impression is still fresh in your head.

Social life is busy, and it can be easy to lose track of what is going on. Consider creating yourself a template for your observations, using the categories in Table 4.2 as a guide.

Becoming efficient at noticing and noting down social events takes time and practice. Generating notes and dealing with them can be overwhelming, especially when you have not worked with unstructured data before. To get you started, visit https://observeit. netlify.app/ to access the companion web app for this chapter. It allows you to practice observations from videos, including your own. It also allows you to generate a template for your fieldnotes using Table 4.2.

Analysis

Analysing your notes can be done in different ways and with the help of different tools. Before you can begin analysing, you first need to organize your notes, so that you can work with them. Your notes may come in the format of the categories suggested above, or you may have developed your own way of structuring them. Maybe you have even taken notes that are just chunks of texts. You may have taken notes by hand or in a digital format. If you are overwhelmed by your notes, you might find it helpful to use the online tool for this chapter to generate a file for you that you can further work with in a program like Microsoft Excel, NVivo, or ATLAS.ti. However, if you prefer to work with pen and paper, you might want to spread your notes out on the floor and work with your notes like that. Before you get into identifying themes for your analysis, and reduce the data you are working with, you will be expanding your notes to help you gain a better understanding of what is going on.

TABLE 4.2 Observation Categories

Category	Includes	You Should Note
Appearance	Clothing, age, gender, physical appearance	Anything that might indicate membership in a group
→ Verbal behaviour and interactions	Who speaks to whom and for how long; initiation of talk	What are the topics they speak about; how do they speak
Physical behaviour and gestures	What people do: who does what, who is interacting, who is not interacting	How people use their bodies to communicate, including emotions
Personal space	How close people stand to one another	Preferences concerning personal space
Human traffic	People who enter and leave	Where, how long, who they are, alone?
People who stand out	Identification of people who receive attention from others	Characteristics: Are they strangers, do they belong to the group?

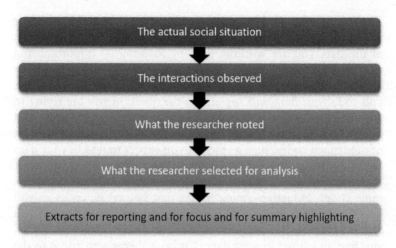

FIGURE 4.1 *Expanding your data.*

Use your notes to describe the social situation accurately, providing detail for the context. For example, if you are observing a primary school maths class, you might not be interested in all of the class but in specific instructions or activities students and teachers are engaged in. Next, describe the interactions between participants that you observed – what did participants actually do? Consider what you noted at the time of your observation: is what you noticed comparable across individual incidents? Do you notice commonalities? What did you pay most attention to? Based on your notes, what stands out to you and should be analysed further? Again, make sure that you take notes on your thoughts. Qualitative analysis generates a lot of data, and it can be tempting to think that you will remember your ideas. However, the intricacies of social life are easily forgotten or misremembered, and later misconstrued in your report. Taking the time to make notes on your data will help you in the next step of your analysis. As you can see in Figure 4.1, we can never capture everything that happens in a particular situation.

After you have organized your data and gotten a better overview of how it is structured, it is time to categorize it further. This step is known as coding in qualitative data analysis. The exact steps you take for it will depend on the theoretical framework of your study. Some approaches, such as Grounded Theory, require some specific engagement with your data, which will not be covered here.

The overarching goal of any form of coding is to assign meaning to similar parts of your observation, which leads to a reduction of the data you are working with by focusing on important and recurring themes. In the previous step, you already annotated your data and identified important extracts to focus on. The way that you code your data will depend on the question you are trying to answer. There are two ways of creating your codes: deductive and inductive. Deductive coding means that you are starting with a set of predefined codes, such as themes you expect to find in your data based on the literature. Deductive coding is useful when you work together with others because you can ensure that everyone uses the same codes. Inductive coding means that you create codes as you go through your data. This format is especially useful when you and the literature know very little about the research area. When you find an extract in your data that fits a theme, you add it to the code heading. If you are doing this manually, make sure that you note where the extract of data came from. Software like NVivo can help you manage your data and keep track of how your data interconnects but does require some getting used to. If you intend to use unfamiliar software in your project, make sure to set aside some time to learn the functions you need for your project.

When generating your codes, try to make them descriptive by using short phrases, instead of single words or numbers. The difficult part about coding is to ensure that you compare the themes in your data, not the wording. Work your way systematically through your data. Do not be afraid to re-sort your data into different codes if you find that your original grouping is unsuitable. Capturing the essence of qualitative data takes time and considerable effort.

Box 4.2 contains an activity to give you some experience in coding.

Box 4.2 Practising Coding

 Have a go at these activities:

1. Look around you and find a range of objects that loosely fit into a category – for example, everything that is currently on

your desk; I like to use collections of chocolate and sweets
with my students.

2. Take some time to really look at the items. What are some
   ways that you could group the items? You might consider visual
   aspects, such as shape, size or colour of the objects; you could
   group them by function or use; you could also create more
   abstract categories, such as what groups of people use the
   items, what does it say about their education, social standing
   and so on?

The activity in Box 4.2 can help you discover whether you have
a preference to create codes that are very descriptive or rather on
a higher, abstract level. Your understanding of your data should
demonstrate that you can both describe it accurately and interpret
it. Make sure that you present your data in a balanced manner.
Coding your data will leave you with a clear summary of important
themes in your data that you can use to structure and write up your
report. You have also generated a list of examples that you can use
to illustrate your points in your report to make data accessible to
your reader.

What Observations Are Not Suitable for?

Observations cannot confirm hypotheses, and you cannot infer
what may have caused a behaviour. The ability to generalize from
your data to the population is therefore limited. Observations
do not help you understand what is happening within a person
(e.g. emotions, cognition or perception of a situation). They
are only suitable for public behaviour and have limited future
projection. It is also important to keep personal constraints
in mind: Observations are very time-consuming, both when
collecting the data and during the actual analysis. Observing
real-life events often also means that you need to consider the
travel time and expenses to your chosen field site. This makes
observations expensive. In some cases, observations may be a

useful secondary mode of data collection method that you could use to generate extra insights in addition to using a different primary method, such as interviews.

Box 4.3 Observations in Use

Observations are often used as a secondary form of data to support a primary data source. In this study, interviews were carried out with teachers and head teachers at various schools. We were interested in how teachers incorporate Fundamental British Values into their teaching. In addition, classes were recorded to compare what was said in the interviews to with practice observed in the classroom. This was especially useful as interviewees struggled to articulate their teaching practice.

Szczepek Reed, B., Said, F., Davies, I., & Bengsch, G. (2020). Arabic complementary schools in England: Language and Fundamental British Values. *Language, Culture and Curriculum, 33*(1), 50–65.

PART TWO

Further Qualitative Methods

CHAPTER FIVE

Document Analysis

Sheikha Al Sheyadi

What Can This Method Tell Me?

Document analysis is useful when you want to examine, interpret and make sense of data contained in documents. Based on your research question, analysing a document may help you to gain understanding of policies, practices or trends in the education system. You can do this by organizing the data you have collected systematically to identify different categories and the relationship between them, using different forms of texts, such as open-ended questions on a survey, transcripts of interviews or the text of a document. This method can provide access to data that would be difficult to gather using other methods.

When Might I Use It?

You can use documents in a number of ways throughout the research process. You can use them in the planning or study design phase to gather background information and help refine your research questions. You can also use documents during data collection and analysis to help answer your research questions. This can be done in different ways: you may review the documents to describe the content, or identify specific educational problems in existing policies, or analyse policy processes or inform new policies. You may also use non-policy documents to examine the implementation of educational policies in real-world settings.

Imagine that you wanted to address the question, 'What is the student's role in a specific programme?' To answer this question, you will need to collect programme handbooks, lesson plans, worksheets, manuals or descriptors as these documents contain information about how the student is viewed. You may also want to conduct a second phase of data collection, such as interviewing teachers who teach this programme, to gain a good understanding of the actual practice from different sources. Chapter 1 explores interviews in detail.

Terminology

Before you move on to look at how to select, make sense of and synthesize data in documents, you need to learn some of the technical terms and keywords used in document analysis, which you can see in Table 5.1.

TABLE 5.1 Document Analysis Vocabulary

Term	Meaning
Coding	The process of organizing your collected data or observations into a set of categories.
Code	A statement/phrase/word which represents a single idea.
Category	The collection of data that appear to deal with the same issue in the same place.
Reflexivity	The examination of your own beliefs and judgements in the research process.
Peer debriefing	Occurs when you seek support from another researcher willing to provide guidance and feedback. It provides you with the opportunity to assess whether or not the findings make sense based on your raw data.
Saturation	The point at which sampling more data will not lead to more information related to research questions.

Data Analysis Process

Analysing and interpreting data in your documents requires bringing understanding. You may be asking yourself the following questions: How do I start? What information do I need? How much information do I need? How many documents do I collect?

You will need a step-by-step guide to help you analyse your documents – see Box 5.1. You will probably use the following phases:

1. Getting to know the data
2. Focusing the analysis
3. Creating code categories
4. Interpretation – bringing it all together

Box 5.1 Top Tip: Reporting Your Method

You are not required to follow these steps too rigidly. Remember, describing your method helps you in the process of making sense of your data and supports your study's trustworthiness.

We will use the example given above to work through this process.

In Step 1, you need to decide on the nature and the number of documents (approximately) you plan to analyse. You also need to decide on a list of places to search for documents (online search, school archives or other databases). Depending on your research focus, you may review a handful of documents if you focus on a programme or a single educational policy. However, you may look at hundreds of documents if you focus on educational issues or multiple policies. You may use different types of documents, such as formal documents (laws or official policies), institutional materials (reports or evaluations) and informal materials (meeting notes or presentations). During this initial step, it is useful to devise a file-naming system for your documents (e.g. Topic.Author.Date.

Institution.), so you can retrieve your documents easily throughout the process of your research.

Once you consider the number of documents you will analyse, familiarize yourself with the data contained in these documents. Perhaps print them out for reading and re-reading, and write down your initial impressions. You will return to your initial notes when you start analysing your data.

In Step 2, review the purpose of the analysis and what it is intended to find out. You may review your key questions. You will want to consider your own position towards the documents; it may be helpful to keep a 'reflexivity' memo documenting how your personal views might influence your analysis.

While analysing your data, it is important that you minimize or avoid bias. You need to remain aware of your own personal assumptions and beliefs, previous experiences and knowledge and professional background. For example, did the data in a specific document feel different from what you were expecting? Were you influenced by your prior knowledge and did you use such knowledge when interpreting your data? Take note of your beliefs and judgements and remember to write these down (see Box 5.2). These notes will probably be helpful at a later stage in the analysis when the meaning becomes clear. Be open to finding new ideas and perspectives.

Box 5.2 Top Tip: Keeping Track

To help you keep focused during analysis, write down your research aim and questions on a sheet of paper or sticky note and keep it nearby as you work.

Now ask yourself, how can I organize these data in the most coherent manner? What are my priority categories? You should read for overall meaning as you search for data related to your research questions.

Step 3: As you go along, you will begin to observe and learn from the data. Data can be analysed using either an inductive or a deductive approach. For the inductive approach, close reading of the document and seeing similar phrases and repeated word patterns allows you to create categories from the data itself. This may, in some cases, lead to subcategories being recognized within your categories. In the deductive approach, however, you establish categories based on your theoretical framework. Then sort your data into those predetermined categories.

You will probably make notes or highlight on the documents themselves, but you may also use an Excel spreadsheet, where you list the documents in rows and put the categories in columns, and copy the details into the appropriate cells. Another method is to import your documents into coding software such as ATLAS.ti or NVivo to assist data analysis, but you will need to ask your supervisor about this.

In our example, we have identified two approaches to examining views about the student role in a programme: teacher centred and student centred. These two approaches are the main categories we will use for the analysis, and they are abbreviated as TC and SC, respectively. Each of these categories includes different beliefs about how students are viewed, as shown in Figure 5.1.

In this example,

1. the top-level code describes the topic (the role of the student);
2. the mid-level code specifies whether the student is viewed from a TC or SC perspective; and
3. the third level details the attributes associated with the topic.

This step involves reading and re-reading the texts in order to decide where to classify different codes. As you read more documents, you

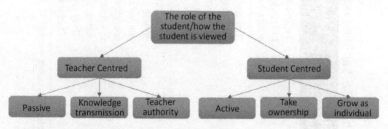

FIGURE 5.1 *Examples of levels of coding.*

TABLE 5.2 Sample Coding

Categories (Approaches)	Passages	How the Student Is Viewed
TC	'I think it's pretty easy to determine that most students aren't ready to perform on an academic level.'	Students are viewed as lacking knowledge which needs to be transmitted to them before they move to the next level.
SC	'The emphasis is on the types of experiences that students must have.' 'To shape developed and well-rounded individuals whose potential is enhanced to the fullest.'	The teacher or the institution provides students with learning experiences and allows them to grow through these experiences.
TC and SC	'The HEI's approach to teaching and learning enables students: to develop as independent learners, ... and to develop their capacity for analytical, critical and creative thinking ... to ensure students are able to develop as learners' 'They are stimulated to think out of the box.' 'Students are involved in discussions.'	Students are encouraged to develop and grow as individuals and to think critically.

Note: SC, student centred; TC, teacher centred.

may need to go back and seek further information to capture all the relevant details, and you may find that some data may fit into more than one category or subcategory. Table 5.2 shows an example of this process.

During the process of coding, you may find that some words are confusing and very hard to classify. These problematic words do not seem to fit any of the identified categories. In order to deal with the problematic words issue, try group examples of these words. This should help you decide what to include and what to exclude and where to classify certain statements/words.

Once coding is complete, you can see the full picture. Are these documents enough? What is missing? Are there observations that stand out in these documents? What else do you notice? You will know you have completed your document review when saturation happens. This means that you have sufficiently understood the topic you are studying and you feel confident you have found good answers to your research questions, and that you will not gain anything further from continuing your analysis.

To determine whether your coding makes sense, it is advantageous to send your data for peer debriefing. You can compare your analysis with coding done by another researcher on a sample of the same data. Have you identified the same references? Do you agree on coding? Do you agree on categories? You can discuss and reflect together in order to agree on the best way forward in your data analysis.

In order to highlight patterns in your codes in and between documents, it is useful to count the number of references for each category. These counts are not suited to statistical analysis, but they can provide you a very rough estimate of relative importance and they can reveal general patterns in the data. Thus, based on these counts, in our example, you could tell which approach is emphasized the most.

Step 4 is about interpreting the data and attaching meaning and significance to what you have found. As a result of categorizing and sorting the data, you will notice that a list of important findings is beginning to develop. In order to present the results about the views about student role among participants, Venn diagrams and bar charts can be used. These visual displays will help you communicate your findings. You can also use descriptive examples and quotes to illustrate the points and to bring data to life.

Other than presenting the findings and showing whether or not the participants and documents were similar or different in their views, Venn diagrams and bar charts help to present fuzziness described in terms of the overlapping approaches. They show clearly where the references are placed.

As you can see, the process of document analysis requires a lot of thought. Data analysis takes time. It may take weeks and can be demanding and complex. You need time to read, grasp the meaning, think, reflect and review your analysis. Have faith! It will happen gradually, but eventually it will become clear!

What This Method Is Not Suitable for?

Documents may not perfectly provide all of the necessary information required to answer your research question. You can use document analysis to enhance the effectiveness of other research methods such as interviews and observations. For example, if you wanted to investigate the actual classroom practices, you may need to interview teachers and students to understand the situation. Documents can be used in this case to validate the obtained data.

CHAPTER SIX

Discourse Analysis

Asadullah Lashari

What Can This Method Tell Me?

Discourse analysis (DA) is a method or tool to study written or spoken language in use. It helps us to examine underlying meanings generated from how people use language and why they use certain words or structures in a particular context. In other words, DA is the study of language and its relationship with the particular social and cultural context in which it is used. It informs us how the use of language creates different world views and different understandings. Moreover, it also informs us how different identities and relationships are created through language.

Terminology

DA is a specialist field of analysing data. Therefore, it is important to learn some basic terminology related to the field, as shown in Table 6.1. These technical terms are very commonly used in the research in DA, and that is why you are needed to know and understand them.

TABLE 6.1 Discourse Analysis Terminology

Term	Meaning
Context	Context is the setting in which something occurs or happens. Every spoken and written discourse has a context, and discourse analysis is the study of language in context.
Cohesion	Cohesion means linking together. Linguistically, cohesion is a technique in which lexical and syntactic elements combine to generate meaning of a text.
Coherence	Coherence is a linguistic tool through which a group of sentences or an entire text are connected to create meaning. Coherence in text or talk makes it easier for the reader to make sense of it as a whole.
Discourse community	A discourse community is a group of people who share the same values, beliefs and customs and use the same communication norms to convey those with each other. Some of the words used and their meanings might be particular to that discourse community
Foregrounding	Foregrounding is a technique through which a writer or speaker tries to focus on a specific part of the sentence to convey a specific message.

When Might I Use It?

When you are focussing on understanding the purposes of different types of language and their effects, you can use DA. DA studies language with respect to rules of communication. It notes how social and cultural norms are communicated through language. On the one hand, you might use DA when you want to study how language generally functions and, on the other, when you find meaning constructed through language in context. It not only studies verbal expression, but also non-verbal expression of language (these are discussed in the following sections in this chapter). The main purpose behind DA is to understand social communication.

You can use DA to understand all kinds of texts, including

- Books, magazines, newspapers
- Brochures, advertisements, leaflets

- Official documents, reports
- Social media posts and comments, blogs, websites
- Interviews, conversation, discussions.

DA as a theory and method has grown exponentially over the years. Some of the commonly used methods of DA are explained below with examples and activities.

Genre Analysis

In genre analysis, the analyst tends to study the linguistic patterns of a genre and their relationship with the context in which it is produced. People choosing to communicate in a particular genre use distinctive linguistic features to accomplish their purpose. We study the distinct linguistic features employed in different types of texts – for example, business letters, memos, news articles, political speeches, literature and travelogues. Each of these genres has its own language conventions, such as vocabulary, structure and rhetoric principles which are known and accepted in that genre's community (writers and readers). For example, you can easily find differences in types of language used between a poem and a recipe, or between a political speech and a travelogue. Box 6.1 presents a genre analysis of the abstract of a research article. In this example, generic structure and rhetoric structure are analysed.

Box 6.1 Genre Analysis on Sample Text Based on Paltridge and Starfield (2007) (Cited in Paltridge, 2012)

Generic Structure		Rhetoric Structure
Title of research article	'A Bordieuan Analysis of International Student's Perceptions, Experiences and Challenges as Speakers of English as a Lingua Franca in UK'	Situation
Subsection of the article	Abstract	

Generic Structure		Rhetoric Structure
Overview of the study	The use of English as a Lingua Franca plays a vital role in intercultural communication globally. English as a lingua franca (ELF) is a contact language between persons who share neither a common native tongue nor a (common national) culture, and for whom English is the chosen foreign language of communication (Firth, 1996). Usually, ELF occurs among speakers whose L1 is different and in the absence of native speakers of English, but it does not exclude native speakers of English completely (Jenkins, 2003). UK universities are hub of international students coming from all over	Situation problem
Aim of the study	the world. The only language of communication among them is English. Thus, language plays an important role not only in their academic life, but the way they interact with other native and non-native speakers of English.	Problem
Methodology	The purpose of this research is to examine the role of English as a lingua franca among the social and academic life (outside classroom setting) of international students. The study is qualitative in nature, and it chooses semi-structured interviews as instrument of data collection. Six (6) international students from different countries studying at University of Nottingham whose L1 is not English are chosen via purpose sampling. The participants who have spent at least 6 months at UK are chosen for this study to get in depth details of their issues related with the use of English language.	Response

Generic Structure		Rhetoric Structure
Results	The study employs Bourdieu's theory of habitus, capital, and field as a framework for data analysis. The findings show that international students with good English language skills have wider social network as well as better academic collaborations.	Solution

Conversation Analysis

In *conversation analysis*, we study verbal human interactions in society. Some researchers study everyday conversation to analyse interactions in an informal setting, for example, between friends around the dining table. Other researchers focus on data taken at more formal settings, for example, in a newsroom or a business meeting. In both these contexts, the aim of the research is to explore how general practices of conversation are adapted to suit the context. These general practices include, but are not limited to,

- Hedging: a word or phrase used to show caution to protect oneself from making claims through less forceful statements;
- Turn taking: a manner for orderly conversation, knowing when it is one's turn, avoiding overlapping in speech;
- Sequence: position of an utterance in a conversation, and its significance in understanding the meaning, and in the social action;
- Relationship between verbal and non-verbal behaviour: non-verbal acts have a verbal translation for the culture they are performed in, and they have shared meaning with the speech community; and
- Repair: when the speaker recognizes a speech error and corrects it through a repeated utterance.

Box 6.2 gives an example of a conversation between host Graham Norton and actor Rowan Atkinson taken from *The Graham Norton Show*, Series 24, Episode 2, from BBC One released on 5 October 2018, and analyses the conversation for turn taking.

Activity 6.1 Look at How This Is Done, Then Try Following the Same Process for Hedging in the Same Conversation

You can also study the same conversation at linguistic and semantic levels. This is discussed in the next section.

Box 6.2 Turn Taking in Conversation: From *The Graham Norton Show* (5 October 2018; https://www.youtube.com/watch?v=Il72uEjs4oo).

GN: So what about Mr. Bean? Have you drawn a line under him, no more Mr. Bean?	Both recognize when to take turn
(Audience laughed)	
RA: I, I, You know, I doubt that he will reappear but um, but you never know you must never	RA signals when he wants to speak, by starting with 'I, I'.
(Audience: awwww)	
GN: The people have spoken.	After audience laugh, both GN and RA recognize when the other wants to speak

RA: Yes quite quiet. But you know, you must never say never again, as Jeff mentioned. Yes you must never say never but there does come a point when you feel as though you've done most of what you want to do with it.

[...]

GN: So are holidays a misery? Can you go anywhere?

RA: I can't go to many places where you're not recognized and it's the yeah, the thing I find most tricky is when people don't recognise you particularly but half recognise you, you know, that strange thing where they go, is that? Because it means they stare. They stare a lot and they just look. And I get that feeling, I wish that person wouldn't stare at me so, you know, I'd rather just you know, hold the flag saying 'Yes, yes it is me.' A few years ago there was, I was in a Land Rover parts department near Peterborough, the kind of place you find me almost always. I was waiting for car parts ... and I could see this guy doing that (staring look). And he came up to me after a while then he said, excuse me, has anyone ever told you that you are the absolute spitting image of that, Mr Bean. And I said, well, actually, I am the actor who plays Mr. Bean and he said ha ha ha (pause), (audience laughed) I bet you wish you were. And there followed this bizarre conversation in which the more I try to claim that I was the person whom he thought I merely resembled, the less he believed me (audience laughed).

RA holds the floor during his turn

Textual Analysis

In textual analysis, you study written texts to understand the meaning presented through the structure of a discourse or a speech event. A written text can be studied at different levels, including semantic (meaning) or linguistic (structure) levels. You can analyse the use of linguistic elements like coherence and cohesion, or use of similes and metaphors, or use of grammatical elements like linking verbs. A sample of written text in Box 6.3 shows the use of cohesive devices.

Box 6.3 Textual Analysis Focusing on Cohesive Devices

Educational researchers cannot simply 'read off' the planning and conduct of research as though one were reading a recipe for baking a cake. Nor is the planning and conduct of research the laboratory world or the field study of the natural scientist. Rather, it is to some degree an art, an iterative and often negotiated process and one in which there are typically trade-offs between what one would like to do and what is possible (Cohen, Manion & Morrison, 2018, p. 3).

Read the text above and note:

1. The reference – using 'it' to refer to 'research'.
2. Substitution – the use of 'one' as a substitute for both 'the researcher' and 'the process'.
3. The use of conjunctions – 'and', 'which', 'between'.

You can also analyse the above text on a semantic level. This is done by using different theories to understand the meaning of the text. You can explore ideologies, power relations, gender discrimination and so on, with the help of appropriate theory to support your analysis; you will need to use the literature to help you with this.

Multimodal Discourse Analysis

Multimodal discourse is a type of discourse which uses more than one mode or channel to convey a message, such as newspapers with pictures and bold headings, billboards with text, pictures, different colours and symbols, actors using dialogues, movement and other facial expressions or children's story books with words and pictures. Multimodal DA studies different modes of language, such as text, pictures, symbols and so on. It sees how each mode creates individual meaning and how all these modes of communication come together to generate a single meaning, referred to as semiotic coherence.

Multimodal analysis is carried out by using different theoretical frameworks and can be used to study the language in various situations. Examples include the following:

1. to study the communication (verbal and non-verbal) between students of different social classes in a classroom or school setting;

2. to study how members interact (verbally and non-verbally) with each other in board meetings;

3. to study commercial billboards advertising different products;

4. to study menus and product lists; and

5. to study travel blogs and vlogs.

Working through the activity in Activity 6.1 will help you understand the process of multimodal DA.

Activity 6.1 Multimodal Discourse Analysis Activity

Look at Figure 6.1 and answer the following question using multimodal discourse analysis.

1. What message is being conveyed in this poster?

FIGURE 6.1 *Sample image.*

Source: Photo by Gavin Penor on Unsplash.

2. How do the individual products in the picture generate specific meaning?
3. How are the different modes and pictures, text and colour significant in generating meaning?

Sample Dissertation Project

Suppose that you want to see how male and female speech differs in student union meetings. DA would help us understand the utterances, beyond mere linguistic meanings. For example, we could see whether male and female speech differences are linguistically determined and whether they construct specific male and female linguistic identities. We might design the following research questions:

1. What are the linguistic choices (semantic, phonological, syntactic, semantic or pragmatic) used by male students in any meeting?
2. What are the linguistic choices (semantic, phonological, syntactic, semantic or pragmatic) used by female students in meetings?
3. What are the non-verbal techniques used by male and female students, and how do they semiotically influence overall conversation?

We must also decide on a DA model or a framework that can help in identifying specific linguistic features of both male and female speech. Any DA model is employed considering the research questions in mind, and our project can be studied using different models, such as multimodal DA or conversation analysis.

Once you have decided the DA model or framework, the next step involves data collection. Data collection for this project would involve video recordings of student union meetings. How many recordings we make may depend on the length of the dissertation project.

Once data is collected, it can be transcribed and analysed according to our framework. For instance, for multimodal DA, you will look for specific linguistic features which construct male and female identities in their individual utterances and find the patterns among them. Besides spoken words, you will also investigate the non-verbal features, such as facial expressions, gestures and signs in the entire conversations. You can also investigate how verbal and non-verbal communication (such as their way of talking, tone, posture or overall body language) interact with each other to create male and female identities.

Problems Faced during Discourse Analysis

Here are some of the problems you might face during DA, followed by possible solutions.

Sensitivity to Being Observed

One important task of DA is to study the language in different natural settings, such as discourse in a classroom, in a business meeting or in a focus group discussion on a topic. Observing these scenarios might make participants conscious of their use of language, so they may not act as they naturally would. This problem can be addressed by trying to keep the research context as natural as possible and by developing trust between the researcher and participant. The data can also be collected in the absence of the researcher, by an intermediary, but with consent from the participants.

Context

Context is very important in carrying out DA. Context is the material conditions in which something occurs, and every spoken and written text has its own cultural, social, religious and political background. For example, if you want to conduct the DA of a short story or a novel, you will find it difficult without knowing the cultural and historical background of the text, such as linguistic norms and cultural and traditions connotations and political influence of the age. Therefore, it is important to study the context of the text or talk before undertaking your analysis.

Literal versus Intended Meaning

The units of speech do not always give complete meaning, although they are grammatically complete sentences. People use language to communicate the meaning at different levels. Sometimes people express something which is different from the literal meaning. In linguistic terms, this is called implicature. Below is an example of conversational implicature.

Example: I can do that if you like.

The literal meaning of the above sentence is that I shall do the work if I am asked, but it also implies that I shall do the work, but I might not be willing to do it. Therefore, the above sentence can only be understood in relation to the entire conversation. Discourse analysts are careful in differentiating between literal and intended meaning in the text.

What This Method Is Not Suitable for?

You might be thinking that everything is discourse and, therefore, DA can be done on anything. It is almost true. However, as discourse analysts work at lexical, syntactical, and semantic levels and every word and sentence is analysed carefully, we need to make sure our material is appropriate for this kind of analysis. This means that working with large quantities of data would be very laborious, so DA is not suitable for large amounts of data, whether interviews, documents or any other type.

We must also choose the right theory or framework to address our research questions. DA is not a single theory or method, rather it has different traditions and schools of thought, which have devised different techniques and frameworks to analyse the use and effect of language. Different discourse methods can be applied to a single data set, such as analysing lexicons or grammatical structure, or understanding genre analysis, conversation analysis and so on, but they are not universally suitable for every project.

References

Cohen, L., Manion, L., & Morrison, K. (2018). *Research methods in education* (Eighth edition). London: Routledge.

Paltridge, B. (2012). *Discourse analysis: An introduction* (Second edition). New York: Continuum.

CHAPTER SEVEN
Ethnography

*Ambreen Shahriar and
Asadullah Lashari*

What Can an Ethnography Tell Me?

Ethnography tells us about an unfamiliar culture by understanding the relevant audience, context or process. Through ethnography, specific communities are studied to gain a holistic understanding of a specific phenomenon – a social or cultural group. People's behaviours and the reasons behind those behaviours as well as the effects of social context on people's lives are under study here. An ethnography finds out the thoughts, feelings, behaviours and lifestyle – in short, culture – of a given community.

When Might I Use Ethnography?

Ethnographers start with a big question, a practical problem in the field. Imagine you want to study a storytelling class in a multicultural primary school in the UK. There are different perspectives from which you can study this class, including the following:

1. the perspective of teachers on storytelling in a multicultural classroom;
2. the perspective of children from different cultural backgrounds on the story; and
3. the influence of home culture on classroom culture.

Here, you can see that ethnography can be used when we want to study a particular group in detail. Through this method, behaviours are studied in the everyday context to understand the perceptions of individuals. The group of people under study are connected in some way, as in the above example where our group is a primary school class, with children of the same age group, and their teachers, meeting every day. We, ethnographers, assume that this class has a culture of its own. And it is the uniqueness of the culture of this group that you are interested in and want to study. With this study you would like to understand differentness and reasons behind it.

To conduct ethnographic research on the above project, first you need to locate a school in a multicultural area and then choose a multicultural classroom within it. Box 7.1 gives you the prerequisites for conducting the research.

Box 7.1 Basic Requirements for an Ethnography

A multicultural school that agrees to allow you to observe and collect data.

A sample narrowed down to one class, with children from different cultural backgrounds.

Cultural information for the entire sample.

Evaluation of the time you need to collect enough data to satisfactorily answer the question.

Appropriate data collection tools to use in this study.

Ethnographers collect data through different tools. It is your choice whether to stick with one research tool or go for more. Your choice of data collection tools depends on your big question, the availability of participants, your convenience and time restrictions. However, the sequence of each tool used, in case of more than one tool, solely depends on your research questions.

Once you fulfil the requirements in Box 7.1, you can go in the field to collect data. Different data collection tools are used in an ethnography. The most common ones are discussed here.

Ethnography is field research, which involves direct and sustained contact with the participants under study. Participant observations are the most common method of data collection used. Participant observation involves an ethnographer observing a natural setting either by participating in the activity as a part of the population under study or by actively observing without taking part in the activity. Instead of studying the participants in the conditions created for the purpose of research, an ethnographer aims at direct observation and recording of day-to-day life of the participants in an undisturbed environment in a real-world context. It is expected that such rich encounters would yield in-depth data.

Now imagine for our big question above you decide to observe classes of storytelling. Through this observation you would be able to study the group closely, to understand the situation. You would be able to observe the teaching strategy, children's reactions and scenarios where cultural differences are evident. However, to observe the storytelling class effectively, you need to develop an observation checklist and observe the things that are related to your research focus (see Box 7.2). You can adopt a checklist from previous studies, or you can simply adapt a checklist and modify it to suit your study. You can even develop a new checklist altogether to observe different things related to your big question in the storytelling class.

Box 7.2 Sample Observation for Storytelling Classroom

Children raised hand to ask question								
Teacher allowed children to ask questions								
Teacher asked questions								

Teacher gave comments related to ethnicity/religion								
Children passed remarks related to ethnicity/religion								
Children talked to each other about ethnicity/religion								

Interviews are a common method of data collection in ethnography (see Chapter 1 for a detailed study). Interviews with participants help in understanding the observational data or the context better. They confirm your thoughts and observations on the data and put them into words. Interviews inform you about the culture you are observing. And then, you as an ethnographer very soon learn to separate individual aspects from cultural aspects in the interviews you conduct. For the above project, if you want to know about the views and experiences of a teacher on storytelling in a multicultural classroom, you might like to conduct a semi-structured interview with her/him (see Box 7.3). In an interview, a teacher can tell you about their choice of story, expectations from children, topics to avoid and a lot of such small things that would help you understand the background and the culture before you come to the class physically.

Box 7.3 A Sample of Interview Questions for the Above Project

How do you select a topic?
What factors do you consider?
How important is the cultural setting of a story?
Do you consider illustrations when choosing a book?
Do you allow children to choose books for story time?
How significant are culture, religion and gender for children?
What cultural differences do you keep in mind while storytelling?
Have there been any incidents when children disagreed with the writer/illustrator on a cultural or religious basis?

To understand the views of a group more closely, you can put them into an informal discussion on a topic related to your study. This is called a focus group (see Chapter 2). With focus groups, participants discuss matters with friends or others with common characteristics and interests. This can help the ethnographer to draw upon their attitudes, feelings, beliefs, experiences and reactions to important questions under study. The environment in a focus group is more relaxed, and participants are often more open in sharing and discussing than in a one-to-one interview with the researcher.

For the above project, imagine you would like to understand how the children felt about the story they were told. You can sit with them around a table and start discussing the story. The right kind of open-ended questions will encourage them to discuss the topic in detail (see Box 7.4). They will agree or disagree with each other; they will present their personal views based on their own understanding, their cultural and religious values and their in-class learning. Discussions in focus groups always bring forth very interesting and often unexpected aspects of the study.

Box 7.4   Sample of Focus Group Interview Questions

Who/What was the story about?
Who/What did you like in the story? Why?
Which was your favourite illustration? Why?

Besides focus group interviews, ethnographers sometimes take field notes. These might be based on informal chatting with the participants of the study. However, they always make sure that the participants know that whatever they may be talking about can become part of the data. Even so, participants always have a right to withhold information or even request the ethnographer not include particular information when they see the transcript of data. It is very important to show transcripts of ethnographic data to the participants as they are being studied in their day-to-day life. This is discussed later in this chapter.

Archives are also used by ethnographers as research tools. Access to historical documents is sometimes necessary for an ethnographer when they are studying a group and trying to link their present to their past. Documents provide an ethnographer access that they might not otherwise have to the organizations, individuals and events of an earlier time.

Terminology

It is very important that you know some basic terms related to ethnography. See Table 7.1 for a list.

TABLE 7.1 Ethnography Vocabulary

Term	Meaning
Longitudinal	The term 'longitudinal' describes any phenomenon occurring over a period of time. Ethnographic research is usually longitudinal because it studies a phenomenon over time.
Collaborative ethnography	In collaborative ethnography, researchers explicitly and consciously collaborate with the researched community at each stage of the research process.
Unobtrusive observation	In unobtrusive observation, the ethnographer is not physically present on the research site or intruding into the lives of the participants of the research. It is usually conducted on recorded data – archives, photos, films, paintings and written documents.
Interpretive	Most ethnographies follow an interpretive paradigm to describe the understanding of participants of some ritual, practice, faith or culture.
Reflexivity	Ethnographers' reflection on personal beliefs, practices and judgements and their influence on the research during the research process.

Ethnographic Research Design

Ethnographic data is not collected in a structured way. It is unstructured in the sense that there is no detailed data collection plan set up at the beginning. No definite sequence is followed in the data collection process. Neither are any definite categories pre-decided for interpreting the data collected from participants. Usually, the data includes talking to people about values, meanings and practices – both personal and sociological – and observing and recording them in their daily life to understand actions and behaviours (see Box 7.5).

Box 7.5 Traits of an Ethnographic Study

Real-world context
Single group or setting
Unstructured approach to data collection
Narration, interpretation and description of human actions and
    behaviour

What Are the Potential Problems and Solutions in Ethnography?

Like any other research approach, ethnography has its complications. Ethnographers often find themselves facing one problem or another. Here, we will discuss some of these potential problems along with their solutions.

Activity 7.1 Have Another Look at Box 7.1. What Potential Problems Might There Be?

The first question coming to your mind might be, 'What are the decisions to be made to select and narrow the focus of the study?'

Narrowing the Focus of Study

Ethnographies usually result from the personal life, job experience or sociocultural environment of the ethnographers. Your study will be no exception to that. You usually want to study those big questions which are around you throughout your life – where you know their answers are also there, but you only need a more systematic study to understand them. Ethnographies start with a big question, which keeps narrowing down during the process of research. Ethnographers are honest about this changing or focussing of their research topic.

Biographical details of the ethnographers are an important part of their research. When you conduct an ethnography, by writing about your life, you draw attention to the fact that your study can be affected by your different experiences. That is the reason why ethnographers prefer to write in active rather than passive voice ('I understood', rather than 'It was understood by me'). Also, when you write an ethnography, you call yourself 'I' instead of 'the researcher'. By doing this, you declare that your personality and life experiences significantly affect the selection and focus of your study.

The above discussion on the research being affected by your personal experiences leads to another significant question: What should be the role of an ethnographer?

The Ethnographer's Role

If you plan to conduct an ethnography, you need to decide the degree of your participation during the data collection procedure. The role of the ethnographer is very important when compared to the role of the researcher in any other qualitative research. Often, ethnographers are part of the study – a participant in their own research. At other times, they observe a social context closely for data collection purposes, but are not themselves part of the data.

In a situation where you decide to be among your participants while collecting data, your physical presence amidst the researched population would surely affect your data. Not only that, but your beliefs can also affect your analysis. Reflexivity, therefore, would help you in doing justice to your participants. You do not need to try to eliminate your influence on your study, but rather, be aware of it. Throughout you need to acknowledge your presence and your influence. By accepting wherever necessary the influence of your prior knowledge or your physical presence on your data and findings, you declare yourself as part of your research.

Now let's think about when you should end your data collection.

How long Does the Data Collection Process Take?

As discussed earlier, most ethnographic studies are longitudinal and are completed over a period of time. It may take anywhere from a few days to several months or even years to complete an ethnographic research project. Ethnographic research is conducted in a natural setting, and ethnographers remain on the research site or visit it regularly until they get the required amount of data. Sometimes data collection may get disrupted due to external factors affecting the natural setting.

There is no straight answer to the question of time required or a minimum time for collecting ethnographic data. However, the most important factor is trust between the researcher and researched. To collect data naturally, it is important that the researched behave naturally during the data collection period, and this is only possible if there is trust. Suppose you are collecting data in a setting where you are an insider – at a school you teach in or in a community you belong to. In this case, the time for collecting data would be shorter because you do not need time to build trust. However, collecting data in an unfamiliar setting always takes longer.

As an ethnographer, your instinct will tell you when to stop data collection. You will know that you have enough information to say something significant. You will see after some time that you are not getting anything new. It is a usual repetition of everyday life. That is your time to wrap up the process and move on.

In connection to building trust, another problem that an ethnographer confronts is that of data sensitivity.

How Can I Be Careful about Cultural, Religious and Linguistic Sensitivities?

Ethnographic researchers must remain vigilant to and careful of the cultural, religious, and linguistic sensitivities of the target population. Due to the nature of the study, there is a chance that they will touch on cultural, religious or linguistic aspects of the population during the process of fieldwork. There are also chances of the target population getting uncomfortable or hurt in the process of research.

It is important that you study the sociocultural norms and religious beliefs of your target population before entering the field. You must be aware of the sensitive and prohibited topics and issues within the target population. Also, as discussed above, you must be reflexive about your researcher bias and subjectivity in the process.

Another big problem that you might think of is, how far can you follow a prepared plan in such an unstructured study?

How Can I Follow a Plan in an Unstructured Study?

Like all social research, ethnography includes data collection, analysis and write-up phases. But unlike most other research, ethnography is, in practice, very flexible. Initially, ethnographers go to the field to collect data after understanding theory. They do not go with any specific questions. Once they have some data, they revisit the theory and narrow their focus down. They re-enter the field and collect more data. This time they focus themselves by starting some analysis on the way. Ethnographic research is, therefore, a spiralling process in which data collection, analysis and replanning keep going on throughout the period of research (see Figure 7.1).

If you plan to do an ethnography, you should get into the field as soon as possible. You try to get first-hand knowledge of the field. And when you are slightly clearer about the population under study, you start trying to make sense out of words and observations. You start the process of summarizing, sorting, translating and organizing your data. This gives you a clearer view of the problem

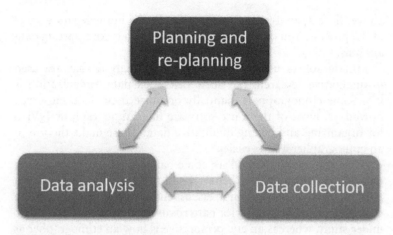

FIGURE 7.1 *The ethnographic process.*

and the population. You get back into the field to collect more data. This time you would be comparatively more focussed. You will have some idea of what you are looking for.

Not only do data collection and data analysis go hand in hand, but some ethnographers start writing up, whereas others revisit the theory at the same time. Once you are in the field, so many dimensions are open to you. You realize it is becoming messy and you need to take a decision to stop, organize yourself and move towards finishing. The decision depends on the amount of data you have gathered, your time limitations and any other outside factors that might affect your study.

Analysis of Ethnographic Data

Ethnography combines several methods of data collection, interviews and observations, and others. Despite getting rich and thick data, often using different tools, there are no specific rules for codification or pathways of analysis. Analysis of ethnographic data is messy, yet fun. You have so much to understand and explore, and you get to see things from a new, often unexpected, perspective. And interestingly, unlike most research, in ethnography you can revisit your data collection site and take more data, as mentioned above. In fact, analysing ethnographic data is not a separate stage of the process. You do not finish data collection before starting data analysis.

Ethnographers usually use methods of analysis that are used in qualitative research. For such vast open data, organization is key. Some ethnographers manually organize their data. However, nowadays, most of them use software like Ethnograph or NVivo for organizing and coding qualitative data. These make the job of an ethnographer a little easier.

After coding, you would see some patterns emerging from your data. A shared thought or behaviour of the group under study is a pattern. Here, it is important to discuss emic and etic perspectives. An emic perspective is looking for patterns as they are seen by the group under study, whereas an etic perspective is how an ethnographer as a researcher, and at times an outsider, understands the behaviours and compares them with theory and other existing literature. A continuous switching between emic and etic perspectives allows us to evaluate the quality of our ethnography.

Like most qualitative research, you will demonstrate how the patterns that emerged from your data can relate to the interpretation of other similar studies and how theory helps make sense of them. You start developing themes out of your data and interpret them. Interpretation of speech, actions and behaviours takes the form of verbal descriptions and explanations, helping to provide a sense of meaning to your data which you can relate to your argument. Ethnographers usually have a theory to understand their data. You will also want to find out whether your data supports the existing theory. It is not necessary that theory supports all the evidence you receive through your ethnographic data. You clarify in your dissertation the limitations of the theory in the case of your study.

Triangulation is significant in ethnography. It validates the data and the research in general. Triangulation is done in different ways during data analysis. Firstly, you compare the responses of different participants: for example, in the project discussed through this chapter, you compare responses of one teacher against another to see if similar patterns emerge from them. Secondly, compare data collected through one source with that collected through another source: for example, you put teachers' responses against the focus group with children to identify how far the teacher understands the children's thoughts and expectations. Triangulation improves the quality of such open and vast data obtained through fieldwork and increases the accuracy of ethnographic findings.

What This Method Is Not Suitable for?

It is very important that ethnographers have access to the population under study. If you feel access to the research setting will be an issue due to your background, (linguistic, ethnic, religious etc.), then you need to address it in advance, because this method is not possible without access. This is often addressed by ethnographers through appointing other researchers who can get access to the target community to collect data, although this probably will not work for your dissertation.

Ethnographies focus on a single setting. Therefore, if data needs to be used for generalization, then ethnography is not suitable. This is because ethnographic studies cannot be replicated and are done to understand the behaviours of small, often less-important groups. Ethnography is subjective to the extent that even doing the same study on the same participants might not result in the same findings if conducted on another day.

CHAPTER EIGHT

Netnography

Kevin McLaughlin

What Can This Method Tell Me?

If you want to know more about the lives that people lead socially online then netnography may be of use for your research project. It can be used to research how online communities interact and the discourse that drives them.

Netnography is an online focused adaptation of ethnography (see Chapter 7), which is a more established method of research that literally means to write about people and their cultures. Netnography is also used to write about people, but instead of using the physical world for fieldwork, it uses the online world as its source of data.

When Might I Use It?

Whether or not you use social media tools such as Twitter, Facebook, Instagram or any of the others that are available, it is reasonable to assume that these online tools have had a growing impact on our lives for a number of years. They have even been used to dictate the happenings on the world stage. Putting such world domination aspirations aside, you can use netnography to explore how a discussion on a particular topic plays out across social media. This gives you access to voices you might not normally hear – you don't have to arrange an interview to get someone's views. Netnography provides an approach to collecting and analysing such a rich source of data, and this chapter focuses on using Twitter to do this. You can take the same approach with other online sources.

Terminology

As well as terminology relating to the social media platform you are using, you will need to know some research-specific terms if you are carrying out a netnography. These are given in Table 8.1.

TABLE 8.1 Netnography Terminology

Term	Meaning
Critical discourse analysis (CDA)	An approach to data analysis (see Chapter 6) that focuses on the style and genre of the discourse; taking the view that knowing who said something and when it was said is as important as what was said. You may use this approach to analysing your netnographic data.
Coding	The process of giving titles or names to different parts of your data to organize it better (for examples, see Chapter 1).
Community of practice	Groups of users that form friendships and working relationships online. On Twitter, they can sometimes be found using specific hashtags such as #Edutwitter, #SLTChat and #Primaryrocks. It is useful to be aware of these communities of practice as they will help you to locate possible lines of discourse that may aid in your research.

Conducting a Netnographic Research Project

Perhaps your project focuses on how social media is used to develop a teacher's professionalism or maybe to analyse the effects the latest education policy document has had on schools around the country. You could certainly use netnography to do this. Box 8.1 provides a fictional example of the kind of rich data that can be found on Twitter and which you might use to explore the latter question.

Box 8.1 Online Responses to a Government Education Announcement on Twitter

@GovernmentEducationAccount: As children return to classrooms after the half-term break, it is important to reporting test results – even if negative or void. Reporting test results is a crucial part of staying ahead of coronavirus.

@TwitterTeacher1: That's pretty poor grammar for the Department for Education ...

@TwitterTeacher2: Please fix this tweet! You've posted it more than once with this error

@TwitterEducationConsultant14: I can't report this because your website doesn't let me so maybe you should sort that out first before anything else

@TwitterTeacher3:

It can be seen from Box 8.1 that an announcement tweeted from a Department of Education Twitter account can be met with negativity. The discourse in this brief section may not be enough to base a research project upon; however, it does reveal a tension between two specific groups: the government department's message to continue the fight against Covid-19 is met not with support but with disdain by an educational workforce intent on pointing out the government's typographical error. This will not be the full story; if you were to read other threads that are part of the same conversation you may find the following discourse being played out (see Box 8.2).

Box 8.2 Online Responses to a Government Education Announcement on Twitter (Continued)

@TwitterTeacher4: This is a sensible step forward and will aid in a full return to the classrooms.

> **@GovernmentEducationAccount:** As children return to classrooms after the half-term break, it is important to reporting test results – even if negative or void. Reporting test results is a crucial part of staying ahead of coronavirus.

@TwitterTeacher5: I agree. It's time to get every child back into school and this will help.
@TwitterTeacher2: They still haven't corrected their mistake!
@TwitterTeacher3: Still nope.

In Box 8.2 @TwitterTeacher4 has retweeted the original government tweet with a positive comment. @TwitterTeacher 5 has then agreed with the retweet and extended their support for it, yet @TwitterTeacher2 and @TwitterTeacher3 have returned to the conversation to continue expressing their disdain for the original tweet.

Designing a Project Using This Method

After you have decided on your research question, you will have to locate those online communities of practice that will eventually provide you with the rich data required for your project. Some netnographers will lurk without actively engaging in conversations and passively collect data, but this approach is fraught with ethical questions that will need to be discussed with a supervisor. A more ethically sound approach would be to enter an online community as a user, revealing your purpose, gathering informed consent in line with your ethical approval and participating in the discourse that follows. However, this approach also raises its own questions regarding your influence on the direction of discourse and whether your participation has an adverse effect on the outcome of your research. Taking this into account, there may be times you may find yourself lurking as well as participating. This brings us to the question of whether netnography is a form of insider or outsider research, and the answer will depend on whether or not you participate actively with the community on the inside of Twitter rather than observing from the outside.

As with any research, you need to be aware of bias when analysing the data collected, and acknowledge this in your work. If you are currently working in a primary school as a teacher or as a member of the senior leadership team, for example, then you may well have your own views on the topic you are researching. Your bias may influence your interpretation of the data collected, so you will need to gather more examples of discourse from online groups to try to get a sense of the wider conversation. However, there is always the possibility that such conversations could foreground those with stronger opinions, whose views could be over-represented. Those who disagree with the discourse may not wish to add their views due to the power dynamics at play in such conversations, which can lead to voices being left unheard or even silenced.

Undertaking a Project Using This Method

So, what does this look like in practice? Let's suppose you are researching the use of #PrimaryRocks as a community of practice by primary teachers in the UK. The following steps will help you retrieve the data necessary for your research.

1. Log on to your Twitter account.
2. Type #Primaryrocks into Twitter's search box and click enter.
3. You can use the advanced search tool if you need to focus on retrieving tweets from a certain date range, group or users or specific accounts.
4. Highlight the tweets you are interested in, select and copy these and paste into an Excel document, using separate columns for the user, the time and date of the tweet, the content and anything else you feel is relevant.
5. Once you have your tweets, the process of coding the data can begin.

This manual process can be quite laborious, so it is useful to know that it can be automated by using tools such as NVivo, a data analysis tool that you may have access to through your university. NVivo can be used to collect the tweets you are interested in and also automate the coding of this data (for further details on coding, see Chapter 1). The following site provides a tutorial that you may find useful: <u>NVivo 11 for Windows Help – Approaches to analyzing Twitter data (qsrinternational.com)</u>.

Analysis

Analysing data collected as part of your netnographic research will take time. You will have amassed a large quantity of rich qualitative data that needs to be read through, sorted and explored for themes and relationships. In the following example, I used Twitter's advanced search function to collect a range of tweets that were posted during a 24-hour period and used the #PrimaryRocks hashtag. It is also possible to use text and word search tools to locate specific phrases and/or words and calculate their frequency. After reading through the results of the search, I manually copied and pasted the contents of selected tweets into an Excel sheet for further analysis. For the purposes of anonymity, you may need to remove any identifiable information from the results, although you will need to be able to track whether particular users tweeted more than once. It may be helpful to give users pseudonyms at this point.

Table 8.2 shows a section of this Excel sheet. Although manual data entry takes time to do, it offers you the opportunity of gaining a more informed understanding of the data you are collecting rather than relying on software to sort it for you.

Coding is part of a qualitative data analysis approach and involves sorting data into themes, topics and relationships. You may find it useful to read Chapter 6, 'Discourse Analysis', to develop your understanding of this approach further.

Having the tweets collected in Excel allows each to be read carefully for further thematic analysis. In Table 8.3, we have marked each tweet according to a predetermined category: positive, negative, sharing, offering support and seeking support. You might also do this by colour coding. This provides a quick visual analysis that can reveal further potential themes and links across your data.

Further Manual Coding of Tweets

In Table 8.4, a more focused approach has been taken to just the text of the tweets, without considering the hashtags or other media. Passages have been underlined in different ways according to the categories of interest – in this case, fear, inquiry and positivity. The columns on the right show the frequency with which those codes appear in the four tweets examined. You could also use highlighters to do this.

Assigning categories takes time, and you will need to go through your data set a few times to refine the ones that are of most use for your research. Emotional categories such as positive and negative attitudes may be a useful starting point; as you run through the data again and again, further categories may emerge. This is all part of a netnographic approach to research; the more you explore, the richer the data you are likely to uncover.

Once you have coded your tweets, you will need to reflect on what it all means. How have they helped you address your research question? What are people saying under the hashtags you have chosen?

TABLE 8.2 An Example of Tweets with the #PrimaryRocks Hashtag

Participant ID	Tweet	Hashtags Used	Other Media
1	If you're having a tough start to the week, hang on in there. You're fab and there are literally hordes of folk who would love to help you if you're struggling. Just ask	#PrimaryRocks #StrongerTogether	
2	We are loving Queen of the falls and it's been great to have conversations today about the characters in terms of digging deeper into their personalities and motivations	#PrimaryRocks #ReadingRocks	Image
2	Is there anyone who has bought the Little Wandle scheme that I can speak to? Thanks	#PrimaryRocks	
3	Great session tonight and a massive thanks to Martin for speaking and sharing some really valuable resources and takeaways	#SaferInternet #eSafety #Teaching #PrimaryRocks	Image
4	I love this sort of mapping – conceptually, children can look down with a birds eye view but also be 'in' their maps – easy to manipulate, change and imagine.	#Outdoor #Learning #PrimaryRocks #Geography	Link

#			
5	Current class favourite book	#SEN #EduTwitter #EduChat #PrimaryRocks #NoChildLeftBehind #ReadingForPleasure	Image
6	A3: I also think we are in an age now where with the internet and brilliant resources shared by everyone that we don't need to be experts and still deliver and excellent lesson. I like this subject leader audit too, could apply to any subject	#PrimaryRocks	Image
6	It's Monday night, it's PrimaryRocks so we need a pre-#primaryrocks question. School dinners have changed a lot over the years. What are your own memories of school dinners? Would you bring any of these (below) back?	#PrimaryRocks	Image
7	Having a student in your room means that you think so much more carefully about why and how you do things. The conversations that you have with them mean that you reflect and improve your own practice.	#ITT #PrimaryRocks	

TABLE 8.3 Coding Collected Data into Themes

Twitter Name	Tweet	Positive	Sharing	Offering Support	Seeking Support
1	If you're having a tough start to the week, hang on in there. You're fab and there are literally hordes of folk who would love to help you if you're struggling. Just ask	X	X	X	
2	We are loving Queen of the falls and it's been great to have conversations today about the characters in terms of digging deeper into their personalities and motivations	X	X		
2	Is there anyone who has bought the Little Wandle scheme that I can speak to? Thanks				X
3	Great session tonight and a massive thanks to Martin for speaking and sharing some really valuable resources and takeaways	X		X	
4	I love this sort of mapping – conceptually, children can look down with a birds eye view but also be 'in' their maps – easy to manipulate, change and imagine.	X		X	
5	Current class favourite book		X		

6	A3: I also think we are in an age now where with the internet and brilliant resources shared by everyone that we don't need to be experts and still deliver and excellent lesson. I like this subject leader audit too, could apply to any subject	X	X	X
6	It's Monday night, it's PrimaryRocks so we need a pre-#primaryrocks question. School dinners have changed a lot over the years. What are your own memories of school dinners? Would you bring any of these (below) back?		X	
7	Having a student in your room means that you think so much more carefully about why and how you do things. The conversations that you have with them mean that you reflect and improve your own practice.	X	X	

TABLE 8.4 Coding of Individual Tweets

		Fear	Inquiry	Positivity
1.	Anyone else starting to get concerned that progression documents for every subject will usher in checklists and data drops galore? Hearing quite a few folk ask about these in all many of subjects.	1	2	2
2.	Can anybody recommend a high-quality class read for my Y1/2 class? Preferably not a book that's readily available/that children may already have			
3.	Look forward to using this next week to support our work on explanation texts.			
4.	I've had a few messages about the templates for my reading lessons! I just thought I'd share some of them in case there's anyone else would like a copy?			

What Netnography Is Not Suitable for?

Like other ethnographic methods of research, netnography should not be viewed as a quick method to gather data from online communities. Although people will have different views as to the public or private nature of their online conversations, a netnographic approach will only reveal what people say in these online spaces and not their answers to specific questions or their private thoughts. Discussions may be overpowered by one voice in the same way as in focus groups (see Chapter 2), and some people with interesting views may not be part of the discussion at all.

Ethical Considerations

You should also be aware of the ethical considerations of using discourse captured from public platforms such as Twitter. Those tweeting may consider their posts to be part of a private conversation, whereas others may recognize that tweets, once sent, become part of the public domain. It would be useful to discuss the ethics of using social media posts with your supervisor before you commit to using the method; you may also find it useful to consider the case study prepared by the British Educational Research Association, which you can find at 'Research Ethics Case Studies: 1. Twitter, Data Collection & Informed Consent | BERA' https://www.bera.ac.uk/publication/twitter-data-collection-informed-consent.

Netnography in Use

Box 8.3 presents an example from a recent article that used a netnographic approach to gather data. This involved two years of active participation in the online community, contributing to conversations and observing online interactions before the researchers decided who to interview to supplement their data for the project. This in-depth involvement with a Twitter community provides researchers a much better opportunity to select interviewees – based on community involvement, interaction and interest – to a research project rather than leaving it to chance.

Box 8.3 Netnographic Research in Use

Netnography is not a commonly used research method in educational contexts; however, it is gaining favour as researchers realize its usefulness when exploring the relationship of online communities and their effects on the real world. In this seven-year study, the researchers used a netnographic approach to explore a community of practice using the #AcAdv hashtag. The researchers also interviewed some of the participants to gain a deeper understanding of how their online interactions and discussions transferred into improved practice in the offline real world.

Eaton, P., & Pasquini, L. (2019). Networked practices in higher education: A netnography of the #AcAdv chat community. *The Internet and Higher Education, 45,* 1–10. doi: 10.1016/j.iheduc.2019.100723.

CHAPTER NINE

Visual Data

Jayme Scally

Introduction

We live in an increasingly visual world. Where once we read our news or books, we now watch TV or scroll through social media feeds. This change in our norms of information input can support the increased use of these same sorts of information for real research data – these are known as visual data.

What Can This Method Tell Me?

Images allow a researcher to explore snippets of reality, supporting exploration of participants' experiences and the ways in which their meaning is made. Visual research data includes things such as photography, film, maps, symbols and art among many other forms. These images can transmit information about the values, norms and practices prevalent in a given culture, classroom or institution, which may often be inaccessible through other means of analysis. Previously unknown or unconsidered dimensions of daily life may be easily captured through visual methods.

If you think about it, when you're in the same environment day after day, certain things will cease to stand out to you. So visual media provide the opportunity for an external viewer to get first-hand observation of the environment, enabling them to call out specific features that may otherwise go unmentioned. Visuals can also allow individuals to communicate thoughts, ideas and emotions that they may not otherwise feel comfortable or capable of expressing.

Visual methods provide first-hand insights into the phenomena or environment of focus (see Box 9.1). Because these can be static imagery – such as a still photograph – we can often expect that they will give an objective representation. Box 9.5 gives an example of a real-life project using visual data.

Box 9.1 Examples of Visual Data in Education

Photos of the classroom.
School brochure.
Photos taken by students.
Diagram of the classroom layout.
Building floorplans, including support offices and classrooms.
Drawings done by students, teachers and administrators.

When Might I Use It?

Visual data can be collected by the researchers themselves. This could be by taking photographs, sourcing existing media, making sketches of observations and so on. Another popular method for collecting visual data is participant-generated images. This is useful when you want to see how your participants live, how they interpret a prompt or concept or what they consider important in a given environment. Visual methods can also help to avoid self-report biases from respondents, which might be found in other methods such as interviews or questionnaires, and to limit the potential intrusion on their lives, particularly if you collect images that would already exist, such as from a class trip or social media accounts.

Visual data can let you see beyond just what someone tells you. Where methods such as questionnaires or interviews can be constrained by the response options provided or by the communication skills of the respondent, images are relatively unrestricted.

If you're working with young participants or those who would otherwise not have access, printing out the photos they create for them to keep can be a great way to thank them for their participation in your research. This can help to build strong relationships for future research or to even develop their self-esteem, giving your research another lasting benefit beyond your actual findings.

Terminology

There are several terms related to visual data that we all know, but some of the more specific terminology is shown in Table 9.1.

We will go over these in more detail below.

TABLE 9.1 Visual Data Terminology

Visual data	Images, still or moving, used in research
Documentary photography	Photos used to chronicle or recount events, commonly seen in professional and citizen journalism
Autophotography or photovoice	When you prompt your participants to take photographs of their environment. You, as the researcher, use these photos as your data
Photo elicitation	When the researcher uses predetermined photos to elicit discussion from participants. The discussion prompted by the photos becomes your data
Video elicitation	As above, but with video

Documentary Photography

Primarily recognized through its use by journalists, documentary photography is the recording of real-life events and situations. Typically, this technique is used in reporting on war or for aspects of social reform. The photographer makes all efforts to be as truthful and objective as possible about the subject matter being addressed. It is especially useful in areas where it may be difficult or impossible to actually speak to those involved in the actual event. Thinking about current events, this could be a good way to study student activism on campuses with issues such as Black Lives Matter or university rent strikes.

Photo Elicitation

Photo elicitation is actually part of a more traditional verbal interview process and is also sometimes referred to as photo interviewing or projective interviewing. Alongside verbal prompts, images are used to guide your participants to share their values, beliefs, attitudes and the like, often by triggering related memories. Here, images are capable of opening specific scenes and events to researchers that they may otherwise have difficulty gaining access to. This also leads the interviewee to share their own personal memories and feelings about the events portrayed and inspires them to share more willingly and with more depth. In this way, photographs are able to start and encourage discussions.

Photovoice

Photovoice is a method used to bring increased attention to a specific issue that traditionally goes unaddressed, typically in working with easily marginalized groups such as those in education, particularly young learners who may still be developing their communication skills, those suffering from an illness or those living in poverty. These people who may otherwise have difficulty being heard are given the opportunity to take their own photographs, showing what is important to them and the concerns they have about their current situation. Through writing and discussions with researchers about the photos they have taken, participants are then able to share their insights with the wider community, potentially influencing future policy development. Participants are able to provide more meaningful insights to the phenomenon, as they are insiders to the situation with deeply rooted experience and information.

Autophotography

Autophotography is conceptualized as a combination of photography and autobiography. Also known as respondent-generated photography, in this technique, the participant is responsible for taking photographs – instead of the researcher – that will be analysed or possibly used in an interview for prompting purposes. This allows for the researcher to view the world from the perspective of the observed. Where this differs from photovoice is that in autophotography, it is common for researchers to give participants general guidelines of what to focus their photography on to help ensure the results are able to address the stated research questions. So this method has a specific target of focus, whereas photovoice wants the participants to guide the focus.

Design of a Dissertation Project with This Method

So, now that we know all the different types of visual data that can be collected, let's see how one study might come together. Everyone who loves to travel, and study abroad is rife for empirical exploration, so let's use that as an example.

As students, almost without fail, are prolific photo takers during their time abroad, this data collection technique fits seamlessly into their lives while still providing valuable information about how they experienced their time abroad. Specifically, the research question (RQ) we want to address in this example project is the following:

RQ: How do study abroad students perceive the culture, customs and traditions of Spain?

Based on the idea that college-aged students will naturally take photos, a combination of aspects of autophotography and photovoice seems appropriate. Remember, used in conjunction, photos and language can complement one another, assisting the participant in creating their responses and the researcher in stimulating additional and more detailed information.

In an effort to lower the burden on the participants, this data collection is presented as part of a photo contest. All students in the study abroad programme were invited to participate in a photo contest where the top three photos, as judged by a panel independent from the research, were awarded small cash prizes. They were instructed to consider the photos they had taken during their time in Spain and identify those that would fit into one of three categories provided for them. The category titles were as follows:

- *Explorando mi nuevo país* or Exploring my new country
- *Cultura, costumbres, y tradiciones* or Culture, Customs, and Traditions
- *Como un español ...* or Like a Spaniard ...

See Box 9.2 for the call for participants and be sure to note the level of detail provided to guide and constrain the submissions.

Box 9.2 Example Call for Participants

While you are abroad you will be exposed to a whole new language, culture and general way of life. You will visit beautiful castles, gorgeous beaches and ancient cathedrals. You will meet new people including host parents, classmates, fellow study abroad students, local community members among others. You will also undoubtedly be faced with many challenges and obstacles to overcome. Along the way you will likely be recording all of this through letters home, social media and photographs. I would like to ask you to look through your photos to see if any represent the following themes of study abroad.

Submit a photo and 100–200 word description of what the photo represents to you.

1. *Explorando mi nuevo país*/Exploring my new country
   What attitudes did you have while getting to know the local culture, language, and people? How did you demonstrate openness, curiosity and/or respect in regard to your host culture?
   E.g. Participating in a new religious service, trying a new food, attending an unknown event etc.

2. *Cultura, costumbres, y tradiciones*/Culture, Customs, and Traditions
   What culture specific knowledge did you find intriguing, exciting, unexpected, fascinating, or even shocking?
   E.g. Ceremonies, markets, holiday celebrations, local festivals etc.

3. *Como un español ...* /Like a Spaniard ...
   What skills and characteristics did you have to develop to behave differently in Spain than you would in the U.S.?
   E.g. Using maps, new transport, engaging with locals, new verbal and non-verbal communication styles etc.

You can see here there is an effort to fit the participants' environment – namely, by using Spanish, their target language, by providing significant detail on each of the categories with guiding questions, and giving examples of image subjects that would be appropriate for each. Participants were also asked to provide a brief amount of text to explain or justify why they believe their submission fit the selected category.

Analysis

As you know, analysis is the most important part of any project. You might also guess that it can be the most challenging part of using visual data. Analysis of visual data varies widely based on the type of data being used.

Visual data can be objective because it provides a still and unchanging image of the focus – for instance if you were counting the number of students who wear sweaters in class – but will most commonly be subjective. It is very likely to be highly influenced by the backgrounds, goals and perceptions of both the participants and the researchers. This is not necessarily a bad thing. Learning about perception can be just as useful as any hard and fast quantitative data you might collect. It really all just depends on the goals of your exploration.

If you're using autophotography, you might have clear guidelines that participants used to complete your task. With photo elicitation you use the images as a prompt for later interviews, so you will analyse as you would any other interview. Using schematics or images of the layout of desks in a classroom, your analysis might be based on measuring the distance between students or how far they are from their teacher. In short, visual data analysis is a complex and demanding process. In an effort to be more thorough and grounded in analysis, many researchers incorporate some element of text when collecting visual data.

Luckily, there are a number of tools that exist to help facilitate this analysis, as shown in Box 9.3.

Box 9.3 Visual Data Analysis Software

webQDA: a qualitative, web-based data analysis software intended for all researchers and professionals conducting qualitative research. webQDA allows you to analyse text, image, video, audio, tables, PDF files, YouTube videos and so on in a collaborative, synchronous or asynchronous manner (https://www.webqda.net).

ATLAS.ti: helps researchers systematically analyse complex phenomena in unstructured data and provides tools that support finding, coding and annotating with primary data, supporting analysis and making connections between them (https://atlasti.com/).

Aquad: The Program for the Analysis of Qualitative Data is a free computer-assisted qualitative data analysis software that supports content analysis of open data in qualitative research (https://www.aquad.de/#).

If we look to our earlier example or photos from a study abroad programme to inform us of student perceptions of Spanish culture, customs and traditions, recall all the detail given to participants to guide their submissions.

See the images and text these prompts generated from participants in Table 9.2.

This level of detail lets us begin with a clear framework that is grounded in the literature on the topic and helps in answering the

TABLE 9.2 Example Visual Data

Category	Text	Photo
Explorando mi nuevo país	My host mom is very talented for a number of reasons including her abilities to knot mantones by hand. Often when I come home she will be sitting in the living room watching television and working on one of these beautiful shawls draped over the back of a chair. I am lucky to have one of her mantones to treasure forever. There is an incredible amount of work that goes into each piece and she sells them so fellow Sevillanos can wear them at Sevilla's biggest festival: La Feria.	~Sevilla, España FIGURE 9.1 *'Mantón'*.
Cultura, costumbres, y tradiciones	This photo was taken on the streets of Sevilla. For me this picture embodies the passion of the Spanish people. They have such a love of life that is difficult to capture in a photo but I feel that this woman's expression gets fairly close.	FIGURE 9.2 *'Passion'*.
Como un español ...	Despite all the controversy surrounding bullfighting, the sport still manages to fill the ring and provide entertainment for die-hard fans. I didn't particularly enjoy the bullfight, but it was a once-in-a-lifetime experience and I am glad I now have my own perspective from this first-hand experience.	~Sevilla, España FIGURE 9.3 *'Olé!'*.

research questions we have posed. Participants were also asked to give a short text statement to justify their submission – this can be analysed using thematic coding or frequency counts, just like any other textual data.

What This Method Is Not Suitable for?

Visual data has been accepted as a norm in disciplines such as anthropology and sociology, though it still faces resistance in other fields, meaning educationalists must ensure this methodology is truly appropriate for their given research question (see Box 9.4).

You must consider your participants, the sources of your data and the context in which it was produced. We are bombarded with visual data – from TV to Instagram, we all use images to carefully craft an idea of what we want others to see and believe. This means that mining sources where the truth is not always the goal could – and likely will – lead to incorrect conclusions from your analysis. For example, using a university student's Instagram feed as a data source to analyse their semester abroad will likely have you believe it was non-stop fun, leaving out issues with language barriers, overbearing homestays or missed flights.

When you are working with this form of data you also have to be aware of wider aspects, such as your potential audience. If you have a visually impaired reader, simply showing a photograph will do nothing for their understanding – you must be thorough and precise in your writing.

Participant-generated forms of visual data may not be appropriate when working in underprivileged communities, at least not without careful consideration. While we take for granted that everyone always has access to a camera via their phone, that is not actually always the case. Alternatively, when you can be sure cameras are accessible, this can actually be a great methodology to use with populations who may not be able to speak or read, as it gives them an alternative means through which to express themselves on a given topic.

Box 9.4 General Opposition to Visual Methods

There are some criticisms of visual methods:

- Visuals are seen as fun, not as serious data.
- We all interpret visuals through our own cultural lenses, influenced by diverse experience, goals and norms, which can lead to divergent interpretations.
- Emerging forms of visual data, such as video, are still unfamiliar for most in a research context.
- The Western academic tradition that prioritizes the written English language is difficult to challenge; visual data are seen as second class.
- Visual data analyses are variable and can be difficult to plan and complete in a way that allows clear and meaningful peer review.

Even proponents of the use of visual methods in research admit that such methods are often unsuitable for addressing specific research questions or adequately answering a question on their own. The methods chosen must be guided strictly by the research questions asked, the experience of the researcher and the acceptability of the technique to the subjects being studied.

Ethical Concerns with Visual Data

There are numerous critiques of the use of photography in research, many in relation to the increased opportunity for violation of ethical guidelines. Institutional ethics committees or review boards are highly attentive to these ethical concerns and their ability to do harm to potential participants. However, any form of data collection has the potential to be intrusive and breach ethical guidelines, so they should all be treated with close sensitivity. As long as the researcher remains cognizant of the risks, any potential harm can be avoided. The fact that the researcher has elicited student submission of their own photos eliminates the potential for many of these ethical issues – namely, researcher biases in photos chosen and opportunity for participant discomfort.

In any instance where people, particularly minors in a school setting, can be identified you must be extra careful to ensure their privacy is protected. This could include deliberately avoiding including them in the images at all, immediately obscuring their faces with blurred spots or blackouts or cropping electronic images prior to any analysis. You also need to be sure to receive full ethical approval, which will be a more detailed process than with many other types of data. Informed consent and/or assent is vital to embarking on this sort of project, so make sure your justification for these methods is well developed and that you feel prepared to discuss it with parents, teachers, administrators and students.

Another common issue may come in the way we tend to use visual media. Think about your own social media accounts. Most likely you aren't posting realistic glimpses into your day-to-day life, right? Remember this with your participants. If you decide to use something from a social media account, you will have to be wary of the tendency to manufacture an idealized picture. The steps you take to select media for inclusion and your manner of analysis will be key for ensuring the integrity of this data in answering your research question.

The use of photography in research brings an enhanced opportunity to compromise the ethical stringency of the project. Most obviously, in many cases, participants will be in the images used, making them easily identifiable. Additionally, when using participant-submitted photography, the research is, in effect, co-opting the work of the individual as his or her own research.

Box 9.5 Photovoice in Use

While visual data in general is one of the less used methods, it is quite popular in many school environments. In the study cited below, photovoice was selected to encourage engagement of the participants in photo creation, to support their reflection on school food choices.

This method was employed to support equity and inclusion to support the students to be the means of bringing change to their school while supporting their individuality and personal autonomy in taking the photos themselves.

This article provides a good example of the SHOWeD method of analysis, where the researcher gathered the participants in a focus group, using the photos as a starting point to ask:

1. What do you *see* here?
2. What is really *happening* here?
3. How does this relate to *our* lives?
4. *Why* does this concern, situation, or strength exist?
5. How can we become *empowered* through our new understanding?
6. And, what can we *do*?

Spencer, R. A., McIsaac, J.-L. D., Stewart, M., Brushett, S., & Kirk, S. F. L. (2019). Food in focus: Youth exploring food in schools using photovoice. *Journal of Nutrition Education and Behavior*, *51*(8), 1011–1019. https://doi.org/10.1016/j.jneb.2019.05.599.

CHAPTER TEN

Think-Alouds

Hassan Syed

What Can This Method Tell Me?

Think-alouds (TAs) can tell us about participants' thoughts, feelings and emotions while they are performing a task or engaged in a problem-solving activity. For example, TAs can help us to identify the ways a learner approaches a task, the types of difficulties they encountered, the kinds of strategies they employed to overcome those difficulties and how they invoked their background knowledge to make sense of the present task given by the class teacher. It may also help us explore the feelings and emotions learners go through during a task. There are two main types of TAs – namely, concurrent and retrospective TAs. In concurrent TAs, participants are required to verbalize their thoughts at the same time as they are doing a task. In retrospective think-alouds, on the other hand, participants say their thoughts out loud after the completion of the task. It is advisable to use TA methods with other qualitative methods, such as non-participant observations (see Chapter 4) and semi-structured interviews (see Chapter 1), in order to triangulate TA data. You might want to conduct biographic interviews before the TA tasks and exit interviews after the task.

Terminology

The definitions of some of the important terms used in TA methods are presented in Table 10.1.

TABLE 10.1 Think-Aloud Definitions

Term	Meaning
Concurrent think-aloud	A method where participants vocalize their thoughts at the same time as performing an activity.
Think-aloud protocol	A document that consists of stepwise instructions for researchers and transcribers about executing data collection.
Retrospective think-aloud	A method where participants perform a task and report what was going on in their mind after the completion of the task.
Reactivity	The effects of a think-aloud activity on a participant. In a think-aloud activity, when a participant is vocalizing their thoughts at the same time as they are reading/writing, they may not be able to properly verbalize what they are actually doing.
Veridicality	The degree of accuracy or completeness of data obtained from think-alouds.

When Might I Use This Method?

What background knowledge was invoked by students to make sense of the text? What factors influenced their performance during the task? Answering these specific questions necessitates the use of introspective tools, such as stimulated-recall interviews or thinking-aloud protocols. The TA method has been used in research in disciplines including psychology, education and applied linguistics, to name a few. Students of education can use this method to explore a wide range of issues related to learners' literacy skills, oral communication, reading comprehension, writing strategies and improving assessment techniques. Different research methods have their advantages and disadvantages. For instance, while questionnaires can inform us about participants' beliefs and attitudes towards a certain phenomenon, interviews can be used to explore and probe into the participants' perceptions and observations can inform us about the actual behaviour of the participants in real time, none of these methods can tell us about the thinking processes of learners at a time when they are performing an activity. As a problem-solving approach, TAs allow us to tap into the process of learning and teaching in educational settings.

Imagine you were to explore the cognitive process the students go through when they are doing a reading for writing task. More specifically, you want to know, (i) the type and frequency of the knowledge (e.g. vocabulary, grammar, background knowledge) and (ii) the factors that influence students' performance in their reading for writing task. These questions can be answered using other methods, such as questionnaires and interviews. For instance, you might develop and administer a questionnaire to ask students questions about what was going on in their mind while doing the task. Alternatively, you might select what you consider to be the most representative sample of the undergraduate students and conduct semi-structured or focused group interviews with them to elicit their responses to the questions above. However, no matter how useful these responses may be, they do not render accurate data since the methods do not provide insights into what each student was thinking while doing a specific reading-for-writing task. In both cases students rely on their memory to respond to these questions. What words and sentences do they find difficult?

Design

It is noteworthy that factors including type of report, language of verbal report or learning task, type of task, participants' age and instructions for the TA task might affect the methodological rigour of TA protocols (Hu & Gao, 2017). Therefore, the TA method requires thorough preparation, caution and time investment on the part of the researcher. Some of the important considerations for novice researchers using TA protocols are presented below.

Pre-task Considerations: Task Design

First of all, you must obtain consent from the target population well in advance. Participants must be informed about the nature of the task they would be expected to perform, the approximate duration of the task, how the data will be used, and confidentiality and anonymity. Studies using the TA method ought to select a small sample in order to obtain rich and in-depth insights into participants' cognitive processes (Cowan, 2017). You also need to think about the type and level of difficulty of a task. Tasks must be chosen with respect to participants' cognitive abilities. Difficult tasks might induce a high cognitive overload and affect the verbalization process, while over-simplistic tasks tend to elicit an automatic response from a participant. Another downside of difficult tasks is that they are time-consuming and require more time investment on the part of each participant. Such tasks might exhaust participants, negatively affect their motivation to either complete the task or continue thinking aloud and, consequently, reduce the veridicality of the TA data. In addition, researchers must consider the instructions that will be provided to participants. Instructions lacking clarity, coherence or completeness might result in participants' confusion and, subsequently, inauthentic and incomplete verbalizations. A good idea is to write down detailed, step-by-step instructions in the mother tongue of the participants and ask a colleague or a student to check them for clarity and completeness. In the instructions, participants must be informed not only about what they are expected to do, but also why they need to do it. For example, instructions for participants for a reading task could be as shown in Box 10.1.

Box 10.1 Think-Aloud Instructions for Participants

You are expected to do the following things while performing the activity:

1. Imagine you are reading this text at home. You may read, think, take notes the way you normally do in your room.

2. *Say* your thoughts, feelings, and emotions while you are reading the text or taking down your notes. Talk constantly and loudly enough into your microphone.
3. You don't need to justify what you are doing. Just think out loud as if you were talking to yourself as you did the task.
4. You may use any language for thinking aloud in which you usually think or are comfortable in thinking. For example, you can use your mother tongue or use both your mother tongue and English.
5. You can use your dictionary during reading and writing, if you want.

Participant Training

Training participants is one of the most important steps in TA research and must be done carefully before administering the actual task. Since many participants are not used to thinking aloud while reading or writing, it is necessary to first conduct a brief training session with them with the purpose of introducing them to the process of thinking aloud. There are short tutorial videos available online, and you may wish to show your participants those videos to familiarize them with the think-aloud process. Alternatively (or in addition to videos), you may demonstrate the think-aloud procedure to your participants by acting it out yourself. In my research into reading comprehension difficulties and strategies of undergraduate (n = 11) and postgraduate (n = 11) students, I conducted separate training sessions with each student before handing them the practice task. Students were first informed about what thinking aloud means. After that, they were shown two videos demonstrating thinking aloud. In some cases, however, I had to demonstrate thinking aloud myself to students. Since the students in my study were university students, they displayed confidence after watching videos. However, researchers working with younger participants (e.g. secondary- or higher-secondary level students) might need more rigorous training and explanation in order to ensure the participants have understood the task well.

Once the participants are ready, they should be given a practice task in order for them to practice thinking aloud. That is, you may give them a text to read and provide them with clear oral and written instructions to follow while doing the task. Researchers should select a quiet and comfortable room for participants where the flow of think-aloud activity cannot be disrupted. Participants must be given the practice task right before the main task, so that they are mentally ready for verbalizing their thoughts and feelings in the main task. It is advised that the practice task should not be too exhaustive for the participants to perform thinking aloud for the main task later on. Secondly, the practice task should be different from the main task since similar tasks might affect verbalization of thoughts because of the readers' overfamiliarity with the text.

Prompting

Reading and thinking aloud does not come naturally to everyone. Most of us prefer to read silently or think silently while reading. In TA research, therefore, participants tend to forget or stop thinking aloud after sometime during the task, and the danger is that they might perform the task silently or they might just say a few TA statements. This might jeopardize the research objectives, render the data analysis difficult and limit the interest of the findings. Participants must be prompted and encouraged to continue thinking aloud. You may want to stay in the same room as the activity is happening to prompt the participants to continue when they stop thinking loud for thirty seconds. However, caution must be observed in this because too much prompting can interrupt participants' train of thought and interfere with the activity. Different ways have been suggested to get around this issue: you may avoid prompting the participants during the TA sessions and take notes instead to be asked in the follow-up interviews after the session. Another way is to place a 'KEEP THINKING ALOUD' sign in front of the participant on the table as a reminder for thinking aloud. Once the participants have completed the practice task, they can be invited to ask any questions they might have regarding the activity they have completed. See the instructions for the instructor, data collector and transcriber in Box 10.2.

Box 10.2 Think-Aloud Protocol Instructions for the Instructor and Transcriber

1. Invite each participant separately for a think-aloud session.
2. Find a place that will be free from interruptions and put a sign on the door. Have paper, pens and everything required ready before the participant arrives.
3. You may use a digital voice recorder or a mobile phone for recording participants' think-alouds. Put the microphone on a towel or quiet surface and test its volume and placement by reading the participant's name, the date and the name of the task onto the recorder. Then test the recorder by playing your introduction back. Cue the recorder to start at the end of your intro. Make sure the device is working properly and the battery is fully charged.
4. Ask the participant to do a short warm-up thinking aloud (see the practice task), then listen for where you had to prompt them before trying again. During the practice session as well as the actual session, prompt the participant by simply saying something like, 'What are you thinking?' or 'Are you thinking aloud?' whenever the participant falls silent for fifteen or twenty seconds. You may also place a 'keep thinking aloud' sign on the table to remind participants to verbalize all thoughts.
5. Turn the recorder on. Stay with the participant to prompt them whenever they fall silent. If the participant mumbles, turn up the recorder and ask the participant to speak up.
6. When the session is over, collect all the materials – notes, drafts and text. Make sure to obtain any participant details you need. Also, make sure notes and pages are numbered in the order in which they were written. You may need the participant's help to figure this out.
7. Finally, protocols should be typed double spaced, no paragraphs, with name and date and with ellipses (. . .) for short pauses and underlined spaces (___) for unintelligible fragments.

Transcription and Analysis

Analysis of TA data depends on the objectives of your study. However, it is necessary that TA recordings must be transcribed word for word. Transcribers need to decide upon the rules to be followed while transcribing the TA data. For example, in a study into students' strategies while reading an L2 text, you need to separate the textual words from participants' TA comments while reading. Textual words can be in bold, while participants' TA comments can be transcribed without bold, or vice versa. Similarly, words repeatedly uttered by participants while think-aloud can be in bold and underlined. Transcriber's comments, additional information or translations from the student's L1 can be given within square brackets. Box 10.3 illustrates one of the many ways of transcribing TA data. This example has been taken from the data collected for my ongoing literacy project. In this example, the participant does the thinking aloud in English and her mother tongue, Sindhi.

Box 10.3 Transcription Example

THINKING ALOUD WHILE YOU READ AND WRITE. Ok, I have to read and write.

We are interested in the thoughts that go through your head as you read and write. We are asking you to do these things: I have to do these things.

1. **Work on the task as you normally would if you were alone in your room:** same as if I'm alone in the room; **read, think, take notes, or just write. However, don't erase. Simply cross through, like this word; anything you don't intend to use.** Ok I don't have to erase; just cut.
2. **While you are reading** while thinking, I have to keep these things in mind **thinking to yourself, or writing – please <u>SAY OUT LOUD EVERYTHING</u>** *matlab loudly sochno aa* [meaning, I have to think loudly] **that you would say to yourself silently while you think, even as you are writing something**

down. Talk <u>CONSTANTLY and LOUDLY</u> enough into your microphone.

In the example above, words in bold are actual words in the text; words not in bold are participants' verbalized thoughts; words repeatedly read aloud by the participant are in bold and underlined; and words in square brackets are the transcribers' translation into English of the participant's TA in Sindhi. After transcription and translation, the next stage is coding and categorization of the data, which depends on the research objectives and the literature a particular piece of research is situated in. It is important to determine a coding scheme – that is, prior to labelling of the data, we need to determine whether to use a deductive or inductive coding scheme. Deductive codes refer to the labels adopted from existing literature on the topic of interest, while inductive codes emerge as a result of iterative reading of data without any preconceived ideas and categories. In our research, we were looking for issues that hindered or facilitated students' understanding of a text. After transcriptions and translation of the data, each participant's statements and responses were separated (note: this process is also known as parsing) and coded applying the labels to the verbalizations that aligned with our research interests. The codes that emerged from the data included, background knowledge (BK), vocabulary (V), and function (F).

Think-Alouds in Use

A number of research studies have used TAs as a data collection instrument. Check the studies given in Box 10.4 for examples.

Box 10.4 Think-Alouds in Use

Think-alouds have been used to support language learners' writing strategies:

Traga Philippakos, Z. A. (2021). Think aloud modeling: Expert and coping models in writing instruction and literacy pedagogy. *Language and Literacy Spectrum, 31*(1), 1–27.
Yang et al. worked with Chinese high school students to identify the strengths and weaknesses of think-alouds as a strategy to support writing:
Yang, C., Zhang, L. J., & Parr, J. M. (2020). The reactivity of think-alouds in writing research: Quantitative and qualitative evidence from writing in English as a foreign language. *Reading and Writing, 33*(2), 451–83.

Potential Problems in Think-Alouds

The problem with concurrent TAs is that talking aloud at the same time as thinking can be obtrusive and tends to increase participants' cognitive load, with the effect that they are unable to articulate accurately what is going through their mind. We call this a reactivity effect. Reactivity effects vary with respect to the type of task and the language of verbal reporting. For instance, research in applied linguistics involving the use of think-alouds for data collection is said to have reactivity effects since the participants were to read or write the text in a second/foreign language and verbalize their thoughts in their mother tongue. Their cognitive load increased, especially in reading and writing tasks, as they had to verbalize their thoughts at the same time as they were reading and comprehending or writing the text. Researchers need to be wary of reactivity effects in TAs involving reading tasks. A strong scholarly consensus is emerging in favour of concurrent TAs. Retrospective vocalizations also yield useful insights into the human mind. However, since there is a time lag between the activity and the vocalization of thoughts related to it, the accuracy of the data might be questionable: that is, to what extent what the participant is reporting corresponds with what he/she was actually thinking at the time of performing the task. This results in lack of accuracy and incompleteness of data. One of the ways to get around this is to get the participants to vocalize the thoughts as soon as they finish the task.

What This Method Is Not Suitable for?

The TA method is not suitable if the objective of your study is to examine the effects of or measure the impact of a certain teaching or learning strategy or a language resource. In addition, the TA method is not suitable if your study aims at collecting data from a cross-section of people for the purposes of generalization. It has already been suggested above that in order to obtain richer data, the TA method ought to be used with other methods, such as interviews and observations.

References

Cowan, J. (2017). The potential of cognitive think-aloud protocols for educational action-research. *Active Learning in Higher Education*, 20(3), 1–14.

Hu, J., & Gao, X. (2017). Using think-aloud protocol in self-regulated reading research. *Educational Research Review*, 22, 181–93.

PART THREE

Further Quantitative Methods

CHAPTER ELEVEN

Reaction Time Methods

Jelena O'Reilly

What Can This Method Tell Us?

Reaction time methods are methods used to better understand how people learn languages (both first and subsequent), how they use their memory, how they perceive certain events or people and much more. In a nutshell, in such experiments, we measure people's reactions to certain stimuli (like pictures, sentences or sounds) and compare them to investigate whether one phenomenon we are investigating produces longer/shorter reaction times than another. The strength of these methods is that they allow us to measure what people do in real time, when they have not had time to prepare for a task. Reaction time methods have become popular in educational research over the past few decades as they give researchers a unique insight into how participants learn and process information in real time, or as the task is unfolding. Participants are not allowed to prepare for this type of task, and we observe their performance or behaviour while they are performing the task. These methods are said to tap into our implicit knowledge or experiences – that is, what we are not aware we know or think.

When Might I Use This Method?

Reaction time methods have been a popular research method in psychology for decades, usually used to investigate the speed of basic thought processes such as making decisions and memory. More recently, in the field of education, and more specifically linguistics, reaction time methods have mostly been used to explore how participants (both adults and children) process and interpret language.

In this chapter, we will look at two types of reaction time experiments, (i) self-paced reading (SPR), which is used to assess how people comprehend language in real time, and (ii) experiments used in psychology (e.g. the Tower of Hanoi [TOHP] puzzle) to investigate phenomena such as problem-solving skills, memory and attention, which are important for the field of education.

Terminology

The key terminology you will come across is given in Table 11.1.

Designing a Project Using This Method

What Is Self-Paced Reading?

Self-paced reading was originally developed by psycholinguists in the 1970s, who wanted to measure how people understand or comprehend language in real time as it unfolds. SPR is typically used to better understand where difficulties arise in sentences that contain some sort of error. These errors can be an ambiguity, an anomaly or a distance dependency. In other words, when people are reading a sentence and encounter an unexpected error (put there by the researcher), what do they do and how do they resolve this error?

In an SPR experiment, sentences or stimuli are presented word by word (or sometimes phrase by phrase), which are read by a

TABLE 11.1 Reaction Time Methods Terminology

Term	Definition
Implicit knowledge	Knowledge that we are not aware we know or do not think we know, and we usually cannot explain it to others.
Explicit knowledge	Knowledge that we are aware of, and we can usually explain it to others (we know we know it and why).
Experimental stimuli	Sentences which contain the phenomenon you are measuring/manipulating.
Distractor items/filler	Sentences that are similar to the experimental stimuli but do not contain the same language phenomenon. Their purpose is to ensure that the participant does not figure out what you are testing.
Comprehension questions	A series of questions that participants have to answer after some or all of the stimuli in order to ensure that they are paying attention (i.e. not just quickly reading without understanding the context).
Reading time(s)	The amount of time or milliseconds it takes the reader to move from one word or phrase to another in a stimulus.

participant at their own speed (Box 11.1). When the participant is ready to move from one word to another, they push a button or a designated key on a laptop, repeating this process until the stimulus comes to an end. The software used to run this experiment measures in milliseconds how quickly people press the button – that is, move from one word to another. Usually, an increase in reading times (more milliseconds) indicates that the participant has encountered the error and is processing it.

Box 11.1 Example of a Stimulus Presented One Word at a Time

+
He
saw
a
girl
cross
the
street.

With Whom and When Can It Be Used?

SPR can be used to investigate a wide range of phenomena, particularly in language, with both first and second/foreign language speakers and with both typical and atypical language development. It can be used with both adults and children. For example, you may choose to investigate how non-native speakers of English comprehend English pronoun gender in real time. Another idea could be to compare typically developing children to children with specific language impairment and see how each group comprehends relative clauses in English (or other languages). Box 11.2 provides a more detailed example of an SPR study investigating grammar processing in non-native speakers of English.

Box 11.2 Example Study Using SPR

In their 2013 study, Pliatsikas and Marinis investigated whether irregular and regular English past tense verbs are processed in a similar manner. In English, the past tense is formed either by adding -ed to the verb (talk-ed) or is an irregular form (drew), and it has been suggested in previous research that second language learners do not process these in the same way. The authors used an SPR experiment and presented the participants with a total of 210 sentences (120 experimental stimuli, 80 fillers and 10 practice items). Below is an example of the experimental stimuli, which appear in four conditions. The first two sentences used a regular and irregular English verb in the past tense, while sentences 3 and 4 used a non-word (a word that is not real) but was presented to resemble either the regular or irregular past tense verb form (Pliatsikas & Marinis, 2013, p. 954):

1. Regular: The head teacher/gave a prize/to the student because she/**helped**/a poor guy/last month.
2. Irregular: The enemies/were scared by/our soldiers who/**fought**/very bravely/and won the battle.
3. Regularized: Aunt Tina/felt really sad/when her husband/**taked**/his stuff/and left home.
4. Irregularized: The babysitter/was so scared/by the noise that she/**drep**/the plate/with the baby food.

In this particular experiment, the sentences were presented phrase by phrase, as indicated by the slash. Only the critical segment (the verb) was presented on its own. There were three groups of participants in this experiment: a control group of native speakers of English, Greek second-language learners of English who lived in an English-speaking country and Greek second-language learners of English who lived in Greece. The results of this study showed that both native speakers and second-language speakers of English processed regular past tense verbs more slowly (higher reaction times) than the irregular verbs.

1. How long do you think it took the participants to read 210 sentences? Do you think this is a reasonable amount of time? What happens if the participants get tired?
2. Why do you think the researchers chose to include non-words in their experiment?
3. Why do you think it takes people longer to process a regular than an irregular verb?

Designing Your Own SPR Study

Step 1: Choose a Phenomenon to Study (e.g. an Aspect of Language Acquisition or Development)

When choosing a phenomenon to study, we usually start by conducting a literature search. In other words, we search for and read previous studies that have explored a particular topic. At first, we might have several phenomena in mind that we want to study, but a good literature review should help us narrow down our focus.

Step 2: You Are Encouraged to (Semi)Replicate Previous Research and Use Existing Experimental Stimuli in Your Own Study

Designing an SPR study, especially the stimuli, is not an easy task, and it can be rather time-consuming. This is why you are encouraged to use stimuli that have already been used in previous research. Many studies nowadays include their stimuli in the published paper, and you can use them for free as long as you appropriately reference the authors. If needed, you can change (adapt) the stimuli to better suit your needs (this usually involves minor tweaks such as changing some of the wording, reducing/increasing the number of items, etc.).

Step 3: Create Your Experiment Using Appropriate Software

One such software is PsychoPy (see Figure 11.1), and its advantage is that it is online and free to use. PsychoPy is available to download for free here: https://www.psychopy.org/download.html. There are plenty of user guides on the PsychoPy website that will guide you step by step to build your experiment. You can start with this Getting Started section: https://www.psychopy.org/gettingStarted.html.

You need to design your experiment carefully; Box 11.3 gives you some points to think about.

Box 11.3 How Many Items Do You Need?

Experimental stimuli: It is suggested that if you are testing two conditions you have sixteen to twenty-four stimuli, or for four conditions thirty-two to forty-eight. In the example above, the authors had four conditions, and would thus need thirty-two to forty-eight stimuli.

Distractors: You can choose to have a distractor item after every stimulus or some of the experimental stimuli.

Comprehension questions: You can choose to have a comprehension question after every stimulus or some of the experimental stimuli.

Tip: If your only goal is to keep participants stimulated and paying attention, you do not need a distractor and/or comprehension question after every experimental stimulus.

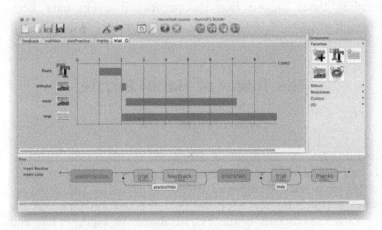

FIGURE 11.1 *Example of the PsychoPy interface (from the PsychoPy website).*

Step 4: Analyse Your Data

What type of statistical analysis you will use depends on your research question(s) and is best discussed with your supervisor. However, regardless of which statistical analysis you conduct, there are several steps that should be taken before analysis to 'clean' the data. First, you will want to consider what to do with items followed by an incorrectly answered comprehension question, as a wrong answer to the comprehension question indicates a lack of attention on the participant's part. There are two ways in which we usually deal with incorrect comprehension questions: (i) we remove the whole item from analysis or (ii) we calculate an average percentage of all correctly answered comprehension questions in the whole experiment for a particular participant, and if the percentage falls below a cut-off point (usually determined by the researcher), the participant is removed from the analysis.

Second, we want to remove stimuli with extreme reading times. It is suggested that stimuli to which participants took below 100 ms and above 2,000 ms to read should be removed. Extreme reading times suggest that the participant might have been reading too fast or too slowly to really process the information in question.

The Tower of Hanoi Puzzle

What Is the TOHP?

In addition to investigating language, reaction time methods have been used in various aspects of psychology to investigate phenomena such as memory, attention, planning and problem-solving, which are relevant to the field of education. One example of such experiments is the TOHP, shown in Figure 11.2, and used to study planning and problem-solving strategies. In this computer task, participants are presented with three pegs, one of which (the far left one) has three discs of different sizes. The participant needs to move these discs to the far right peg while satisfying two conditions: only one disc can be moved at one time

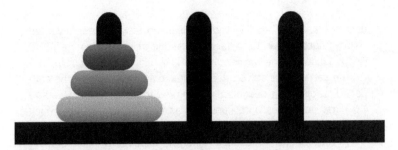

FIGURE 11.2 *Example of the Tower of Hanoi puzzle.*

and larger discs cannot be placed on smaller discs. The goal is to move the pegs as quickly as possible with as few moves and errors as possible.

With Whom and When Can It Be Used?

The TOHP can be used to investigate planning, problem-solving and skill learning with a wide range of participants, including both children and adults. It can also be used to investigate differences between typically and atypically developing children and adults (see the example study in Box 11.4). For example, in a classic experiment, Byrnes and Spitz (1979) used TOHP to test problem-solving skills in children aged six to eighteen years as well as in university students. The results suggest that children's problem-solving skills increase (they become faster and more accurate) in two transition periods, between the ages of seven and nine years and eleven and fourteen years.

Box 11.4 Example Study Involving the TOHP Task

A study by Vakil, Lowe and Goidfus (2015) investigated the associations between reading ability and skill learning in children diagnosed with developmental dyslexia (DD) and those without a diagnosis. They used a number of reading and skill learning tasks to test fifty-three children aged eleven to thirteen years, one of which was the TOHP (we will focus on the administration and results of this test only).

The participants solved the puzzles in a similar way to the self-paced reading test described above, and the computer measured the time (in milliseconds) and moves needed to complete each puzzle (see Figure 11.3). Four different measures were extracted from the results to assess different aspects of the learning process involved in solving the TOHP. The four measures were the following: 'number of moves to solution (minimum of fifteen moves), total time to solution, time to first move, and time per move in each trial (total time divided by the number of moves to solution)' (Vakil et al., 2015, p. 477).

The results showed no statistically significant differences in learning rates on the TOHP between children with or without DD, although children with DD were somewhat slower at performing the tasks.

Time to think (after reading the paper above)

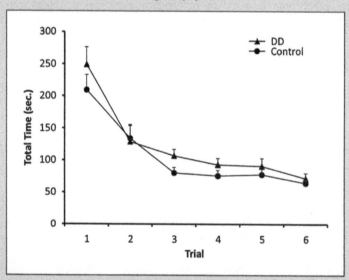

FIGURE 11.3 *Graph showing differences in performance on the Tower of Hanoi puzzle between children with developmental dyslexia (DD) and those without (Vakil et al., 2015, p. 476).*

1. What do you think the authors predicted regarding the association between reading skills and performance on the TOHP?
2. Did the results confirm their predictions?
3. How is this research relevant to the educational setting?

Running Your Own TOHP Experiment

Step 1: Choose a Phenomenon to Research

The design of any study should start with a thorough literature search. Once you have identified a gap in the literature, design your study and think carefully about who your participants will be. You can choose to compare the performance of different groups of participants (e.g. different ages, different IQs, same participants longitudinally (over time)). Will your participants need to take any additional tests? For example, in the study above, the participants took a number of reading tests in addition to the TOHP, but you might already have data to help you categorize your participants.

Step 2: Run Your TOHP Experiment

Running the TOHP task is relatively straightforward as it does not require you to create any materials of your own as with SPR. The TOHP is freely available from the PsyToolkit website. To run the experiment, first download the zip file and then watch a short and simple video on how to embed the zip file to create your own experiment online (see Figure 11.4).

Step 3: Analysing Your Data

The data will be presented to you in a table similar to Table 11.2, with 'column 1' showing time spent on each move in milliseconds (reaction times), 'column 2', the number of possible steps, 'column 3', the number of tries to put the bigger disc on the smaller one, and 'column 4', the number of tries to move the disc where it cannot be. It depends on your research question(s) and the phenomenon you are investigating as well as how you will use this data in analysis.

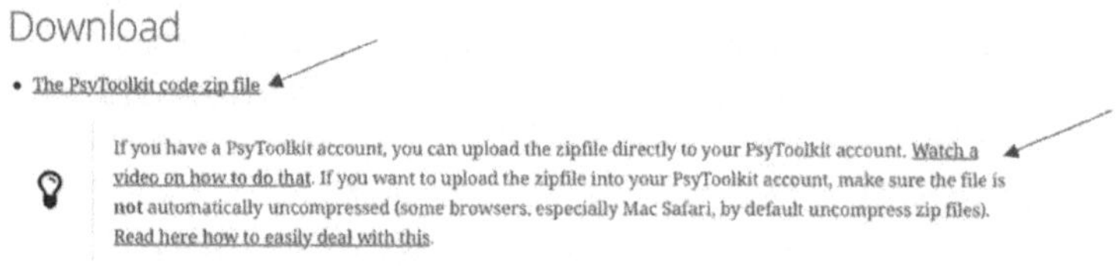

Download

- The PsyToolkit code zip file

> If you have a PsyToolkit account, you can upload the zipfile directly to your PsyToolkit account. Watch a video on how to do that. If you want to upload the zipfile into your PsyToolkit account, make sure the file is **not** automatically uncompressed (some browsers, especially Mac Safari, by default uncompress zip files). Read here how to easily deal with this.

FIGURE 11.4 *Screenshot from the PsyToolkit website.*

TABLE 11.2 Example of Data after Completed Experiment in PsyToolkit

Column 1	Column 2	Column 3	Column 4
2133	1	0	0
3214	2	0	0
4468	3	0	0
5884	4	0	0
7009	5	0	0
8357	6	0	0
9939	7	0	0

Some researchers choose to calculate a performance score based on how many moves it took the participants to complete each task (e.g. Byrnes & Spitz, 1979), while other researchers calculate a number of different scores which reflect the learning process (e.g. Vakil et al., 2015). Talk to your supervisor to determine which data analysis strategy is best suited to your study.

> Tip: Have a look at the PsyToolkit website for a number of other experiments, many of which are reaction time based (e.g. Visual search) and have an application to education.

What Is This Method Not Suitable for?

Because reaction time methods collect real-time data, they are not suitable for collecting retrospective data or for tasks that participants have had time to prepare for. It is very important to ensure that during the experiment, the participants are seeing the stimuli for the first time.

Additionally, reaction time methods are probably not suitable if you are looking to collect data very quickly (e.g. because you have a tight deadline or not enough resources). Setting up and running a reaction time experiment will take a bit of preparation and time, but it is worth doing if this is the best method for answering your research question(s). This also depends partly on which specific method you choose. As mentioned in the chapter, for example, an SPR experiment will take a bit longer to set up and run than the TOHP. So in addition to carefully choosing your topic and the appropriate reaction time method, do take into consideration how much time you have available to set up your experiment and collect data.

References

Byrnes, M. M., & Spitz, H. H. (1979). Developmental progression of performance on the Tower of Hanoi problem. *Bulletin of the Psychonomic Society*, *14*(5), 379–81. https://doi.org/10.3758/BF0 3329485.

Pliatsikas, C., & Marinis, T. (2013). Processing of regular and irregular past tense morphology in highly proficient second language learners of English: A self-paced reading study. *Applied Psycholinguistics*, *34*(5), 943–70. http://www.journals.cambridge.org/abstract_S014271641 2000082.

Vakil, E., Lowe, M., & Goldfus, C. (2015). Performance of children with developmental dyslexia on two skill learning tasks – serial reaction time and Tower of Hanoi puzzle: A test of the specific procedural learning difficulties theory. *Journal of Learning Disabilities*, *48*(5), 471–81. https://doi.org/10.1177/0022219413508981.

CHAPTER TWELVE

Experimental Designs

Verónica García-Castro

What Can They Tell Me?

There are different ways to conduct quantitative research. One of those ways is testing hypotheses through experiments that have been carefully planned and designed. The results of the design process are what we call *experimental designs*. Thus, experimental designs are a research approach used to test hypotheses. They are part of a systematic, controlled and precise process of conducting quantitative research. We use experimental designs to find out whether a dependent variable changes due to the influence or the effect of an independent variable. For example, we can conduct an experiment to determine whether pre-existing vocabulary knowledge (the independent variable) facilitates the learning of new words (the dependent variable). Based on previous research, we can hypothesize that students' word learning increases depending on their pre-existing vocabulary knowledge, but we need to conduct an experiment to determine whether that's the case for the specific population we are interested in.

Experimental designs may also tell us, for example, whether a teaching intervention on reading skills (the independent variable) has an effect on (changes) students' scores on a reading test (the dependent variable). We can hypothesize that receiving a teaching intervention on the use of reading skills influences students' scores on a reading test, but once again, we would need to conduct an experiment to test whether that hypothesis is confirmed for the set of participants we want to test. In experimental designs, we test and compare participants via creating a group of people who will receive the experiment (the experimental group) and a group who will not receive the experiment (control group), so we can compare them and determine the possible effectiveness of the experimental condition.

As you can see from the two examples mentioned above, which are just two of many (see Box 12.1 for more), in the field of education, we can conduct a variety of teaching and linguistic experiments. Hence, one of the advantages of using experimental designs and their beauty is that we can experiment on innumerable topics in the field of education. The first key step to successful experimental designs is to decide on a topic that you are interested in and that you want to research experimentally.

Box 12.1 Examples of Possible Experiments in Educational Research

1. teaching experiment examining whether teaching the relationship between letters and sounds boosts children's literacy skills;
2. teaching experiment identifying whether using art to teach human rights increases students' awareness of social issues in their surroundings;
3. linguistic experiment using comic strips to determine whether they improve students' oral skills in a foreign language; and
4. linguistic experiment employing social media in classroom settings to enhance students' writing skills in a foreign language.

When Might I Use It?

Experimental designs are invaluable methodological tools when you want to test a hypothesis by either rejecting or confirming it. You confirm a hypothesis when, via an experiment, you demonstrate that it was true for a specific population. Suppose that you are interested in conducting the teaching experiment in Example 2 (in Box 12.1). Your hypothesis is that reading short stories twice per week outside the classroom facilitates students' reading comprehension processes. So you design an experiment to identify whether reading short stories outside the classroom actually does facilitate students' reading comprehension processes. You conduct the experiment and discover that, indeed, reading short stories twice per week outside the classroom facilitates students' reading comprehension processes, thereby confirming that your hypothesis is true for the group of students you tested. If the experiments' results had demonstrated that reading short stories twice per week outside the classroom does not facilitate students' reading comprehension processes, your hypothesis would have been falsified and, consequently, rejected. The process of rejecting and confirming hypotheses is what gives life to experimental designs.

You would definitely use experimental designs in the teaching experiment mentioned above because you wanted to know whether reading short stories (the independent variable) changes the reading comprehension processes (the dependent variable). There are numerous topics in the field of education that you can test using experimental designs, and there are also different types of experiments that we can design to test a hypothesis. We can, for example, use a between-groups experimental design where we have different participants in the experimental condition and in the control condition of the experiment.

As you can see in the between-groups example in Box 12.2, the participants in the experimental group are not the same as the participants in the control group. In this type of experimental design, one group receives the experimental manipulation (using comic strips) and another group does not receive the manipulation (does not use comic strips). The participants are assigned to each group randomly.

Box 12.2 Example of a Between-Groups Experimental Design

In this example, the independent variable is the use of comic strips, and the dependent variable is students' oral skills in a foreign language. We might have thirty students in each group (sixty participants in total).

There are some cases in which participants cannot randomly be allocated to either a control or an experimental group. For example, if the sixty participants in Box 12.2 differ significantly in their oral skills and you randomly allocate them into experimental and control groups, it would be extremely difficult to determine whether the use of comic strips helped to improve students' oral skills because the control and experimental groups had very different oral skills before conducting the experiment. When you randomly allocate participants into control and experimental groups, you are assuming that they have similar characteristics. When participants do have similar characteristics, they can be randomly assigned into either group. However, when this is not the case, you can use a different experimental design called a matched-groups design. In matched-groups designs, participants are matched based on their results on the dependent variable. Let's suppose that the sixty participants from the example in Box 12.2 have very different levels of oral proficiency, meaning that you cannot randomly assign them into experimental or control groups. In this case, you would need to administer an oral proficiency test to match pairs of participants based on their results on the test before conducting the experiment. Once you match participants, you will end up with pairs of participants matched according to their results in the oral proficiency test. After you have matched participants, you can randomly assign the experimental manipulation (use of comic strips) to one of the participants in the pair, and the other participant in the pair will not receive the experimental manipulation (no use of comic strips). Box 12.3 shows an example of a matched design for the example above.

Box 12.3 Example of a Matched-Groups Experimental Design

In the following example, the independent variable is the use of comic strips, and the dependent variable is students' oral skills in a foreign language.

Participant	Pair	Proficiency	Manipulation
1	1	High	Experimental
2	1	High	Control
3	2	Intermediate	Experimental
4	2	Intermediate	Control
5	3	Low	Experimental
6	3	Low	Control

In cases where we need all participants to receive the experimental treatment, unlike between-groups and matched-groups designs, you can use a within-groups design. But why would we need all participants to receive the experimental treatment? Depending on your hypothesis and research questions you may need to reduce the possible effects of participants' individual differences in the results of your experiment. For instance, if in an experimental group, by chance, participants have higher working memory than average, that could influence the results of the experiment. Similarly, if in the experimental group, by chance, participants have lower verbal comprehension than average, that may affect the experiment's results. In order to control for the possible effects of learners' individual differences, we can include them as independent variables in our study if our hypothesis and research purpose allows it. However, it is impossible to control for every individual difference, and depending on your hypothesis, you may need all participants to receive the experimental treatment without measuring every individual difference pertaining to your experiment. Thus, given that in within-groups designs all participants are exposed to the experimental treatment, you could reduce the possible effects of their individual differences. You still may have two groups of participants, but all of them will receive the experimental manipulation. To illustrate, in Example 1 in Box 12.1 (the teaching experiment examining whether teaching the relationship between letters and sounds boosts children's literacy skills), the teaching intervention could involve teaching the relationship between letters and sounds with oral teaching techniques and with writing teaching techniques. In this case, we divide the participants into two groups, but all of them will receive the same teaching techniques.

An important element in within-groups experimental designs is to decide on how participants will receive the experimental manipulation. In our example, there are two types of teaching techniques, but how do we administer them to avoid any learning effects of teaching one technique prior to the other one? If both groups receive the oral teaching techniques first and then the writing teaching techniques, we could find that the oral teaching techniques were more effective than the writing techniques simply because they were implemented first.

Activity 12.1 Think of Ways to Administer Both Teaching Techniques to Avoid any Possible Learning Effects

The answer to Activity 12.1 is actually quite simple: in order to avoid any potential learning effects, we have to counterbalance the implementation of the teaching techniques as shown in the example in Table 12.1 Counterbalancing means to randomly vary the conditions of the experiment to avoid learning effects.

TABLE 12.1 Example of a Within-Groups Experimental Design

	Group A	Group B
First manipulation	Pupils taught letters and sounds with oral teaching techniques	Pupils taught letters and sounds with writing teaching techniques
Second manipulation	Pupils taught letters and sounds with writing teaching techniques	Pupils taught letters and sounds with oral teaching techniques

Design of a Dissertation Project with This Method

Let's say that you want to know whether playing video games contributes to improving students' listening skills in a foreign language because literature suggests that it does within specific populations, but no studies have been conducted with children between eight and eleven years old. Hence, you hypothesize that for pupils between eight and eleven years old, playing video games is an effective tool to improve their listening skills in a foreign language (e.g. Spanish). In order to test your hypothesis, you come up with a research question to help you reject or confirm that hypothesis: 'Does playing video games have an effect on the listening skills of pupils aged between eight and eleven in Spanish as a foreign language?' Once you have your research question, how can you actually test whether playing video games has an effect on pupils' listening skills? A scientific way to test the possible effects of playing video games on listening skills is by conducting an experiment. But which type of experimental design would suit the research question and hypothesis? Supposing that your participants have similar listening skills in Spanish as a foreign language and that they can be randomly assigned into control and experimental groups, you may decide on a between-groups experimental design. As previously mentioned, in between-groups experimental designs, we need an experimental and a control group; therefore, you will end up with a group of pupils who will play video games (the experimental group) and receive regular Spanish lessons and a group of pupils who will not play video games (the control group) but who will also receive regular Spanish lessons. Once you have identified the groups, how will you test that playing video games actually made a difference in their Spanish listening skills? Well, you have to administer a pretest to both the control and the experimental group to identify the pupils' listening skills before you start the experiment (before they play video games) and a post-test to determine whether the group who played video games (the experimental group) outperformed those who did not play video games (the control group). Only by administering a pretest and a post-test will you be able to determine whether playing video games had an effect on your participants' listening skills.

Box 12.4 A Between-Group Research Design Example for the Project Above

Control Group	Experimental Group
Pre-listening test	Pre-listening test
Students do not play video games	Students play video games
Post-listening test	Post-listening test

As you can see from Box 12.4, both control and experimental groups receive a pre- and a post-listening test. When using experimental designs, make sure that the instruments you are going to use are suitable for your research questions and that they are appropriate for the population you are testing. For example, if your population is pupils between eight and eleven years old, you will need a video game appropriate for that population and you will also have to think about how often your participants will play the video game. How to choose an appropriate video game and for how long pupils will play the video game (frequency of exposure) are methodological choices that need to be planned and piloted before conducting the experiment. In experimental designs, it is essential to pilot your instruments and the implementation of your experiment before conducting the study. What does piloting exactly mean in experimental designs? Piloting means testing your instruments, the step-by-step process, and the logistics of your experiment before conducting it with the population you want to work with. For example, in the experiment mentioned above, you will pilot the pre-listening test, the type of video game chosen, how often and for how long the students play the video game (e.g. for two hours twice per week) and the listening post-test. Once you have piloted the experiment, you might need to modify it in light of your pilot's results. A rule of thumb in experimental designs is that you have to conduct a pilot study, like the one just mentioned, before conducting the experiment. In general terms, piloting provides very useful insights and feedback to help you improve any experimental design.

Let's suppose you piloted your instruments and the step-by-step process of how you will implement the use of video games within your population and you modified your experiments based on the results. Now, another question that arises is, how do you decide which students you should assign into the control and experimental groups? One of the characteristics of experimental designs is that you randomly allocate your students in each group, but how exactly do we do this? One simple solution is to assign a number to each participant and then randomly assign an equal number of participants to each group.

Table 12.2 presents an example of how you can allocate your participants into experimental and control groups, and it also shows that each group has the same number of participants. It is strongly recommended to have the same number of participants in each group. Why? For the simple reason that if you do not have the same number of participants in each group, you may be unable to compare both groups of participants, and in experimental designs, we want to compare the experimental and the control group to determine whether the experimental manipulation worked.

Once you know how to randomly allocate the participants in your study, another question arises: 'How many participants overall do I need for my experiment?' The number of participants you will need depends on the statistical power you need to reject or confirm your hypothesis. Luckily, thanks to technology, we can compute the statistical power we need in a specific statistical test, which will give us the number of participants we need in our experiment. A very useful piece of software to compute power analysis is *G*Power*. You can find more information about this software here: https://www.psychologie.hhu.de/arbeitsgruppen/allgemeine-psychologie-und-arbeitspsychologie/gpower.

Right now, you may be thinking that there are a lot of steps to follow to conduct experimental designs, but don't be disheartened: once you have sorted out the methodological logistics of your experiment, you are ready to experiment! It is important to understand that for an experiment to be able to tell us accurately whether our independent variable (e.g. playing video games) is causing the changes we see in the dependent variable (e.g. scores on a listening test) and that there are no other elements causing those changes, it must be well designed. Following the completion of the experiment, being able to infer that any changes discovered are actually caused by the independent variable, and not by any other factor, is called causality, and it helps us by indicating that our hypothesis has been confirmed or rejected.

TABLE 12.2 Example of Random Allocation of Participants into Experimental and Control Groups

Experimental Group	Control Group
Participant 1	Participant 4
Participant 2	Participant 3
Participant 5	Participant 6
Participant 8	Participant 7
Participant 10	Participant 9
Participant 11	Participant 12
Participant 13	Participant 15
Participant 14	Participant 16
Participant 17	Participant 18
Participant 21	Participant 19
Participant 22	Participant 20
Participant 24	Participant 23
Total = 12 participants	Total = 12 participants

You may have noticed that experimental designs follow a deductive process: analyse theoretical accounts and review the literature to develop a hypothesis, design an experiment based on that hypothesis, pilot the experiment, on the basis of the pilot's results make any necessary changes to the experimental design, conduct the experiment and analyse the data; the results will tell you whether the hypothesis has been confirmed or falsified, and go back and revise the initial theoretical accounts and literature.

Terminology

There are some key terms that we must know when designing experiments. Knowing the terms in Table 12.3 will increase your understanding of experimental designs, and they will help you when designing your own experiments.

Activity 12.2 Having the Glossary at Hand, Can You Figure Out Which Is the Independent Variable and Which Is the Dependent Variable in the Following Research Question?

Research Question: Does working memory have an effect on students' scores on a math test?

Analysis

The data collected in experimental designs is quantitative in nature. Therefore, data analysis of your experiments has to be done through different statistical tests, and you may need statistical software to perform those tests. One statistical software that is currently most popular amongst academics is called *R*. *R* is free and is strongly recommended for quantitative data analysis. You will need to get familiar with the *R* environment in order to use it, and it has a steep learning curve. Further information on *R* can be found here: https://www.r-project.org/about.html. Another popular statistical program is called SPSS. However, SPSS is not free, but you may be able to download it through your university. A useful tip is to speak to your department's research team to find out which statistical program they currently use and whether they offer any workshops on how to conduct statistical analyses.

The first step in your statistical analysis is to find out the numerical description of your data by employing simple descriptive statistics. You can conduct descriptive statistics manually, with Excel or with any of the statistical programs mentioned above. Descriptive statistics include the average (the mean) of your variables and/or tests you employed. For example, you can calculate the average of math scores (the dependent variable) and of participants' working memory (the independent variable) in an experimental project on the influence of working memory in high school students' math tests.

TABLE 12.3 Experimental Designs Terminology

Causality	Inferring that the changes in the dependent variable are caused by the independent variable.
Control group	A group that does not receive the experimental condition.
Counterbalancing	Randomly changing the experimental conditions within subjects.
Dependent variable	The variable that will be affected by the independent variable.
Experimental group	A group that receives the experimental condition.
Experimental treatment	The conditions you administer in an experiment.
Hypothesis	An idea that we have about a particular research phenomenon.
Independent variable	The variable that may have an effect on the dependent variable.
Pilot study	A small-scale study you conduct prior to administering your experiment to pilot, or test, the experimental design.
Post-test	A test administered after conducting an experiment.
Pretest	A test administered before conducting an experiment.

To continue the example of whether playing video games contributes to improving students' listening skills, one of the first steps in the statistical analysis would be to identify the average scores in the pre- and post-listening tests. Knowing the average score allows us to identify whether there are any extreme scores in our data. Additionally, we can calculate the score that occurs most often in the data (the mode) and the one that is in the middle of the data (the median) when arranged from the lowest to the highest number or vice versa. Undoubtedly, the mean is the most useful descriptive statistic and the one you should always report.

Once you have calculated the descriptive statistics, depending on your data and research questions, you may need to conduct more complex statistical analyses. Deciding on which type of statistical analysis you should use is a task that you will have to discuss with your supervisor and/or your department's research team.

What This Method Is Not Suitable for

This method is not suitable if you are not testing a hypothesis. Additionally, experimental designs are not suitable for those who are not interested in conducting quantitative analysis as it requires the use of statistics. However, you should not be discouraged by the apparent complexity of quantitative analysis: it is far simpler than it seems!

Experimental designs are very useful and fun, and they give you the option to explore numerous hypotheses in the field of education, but they may not be appropriate for your topic if it is qualitative in nature. However, experimental designs could be used in a mixed-method design in which you employ both quantitative and qualitative methods to answer your research questions.

Conclusion: Where Next?

Abigail Parrish and Ghazal Shaikh

It looks like you've made it! If you've turned to this section, we hope you've found the preceding chapters useful and landed on a suitable research method, or two, to use in your dissertation project. That must be a good feeling!

By now, you've probably done lots of reading in your topic area and got a feel for what other people have done. If not, you should definitely spend some time doing this to help you confirm that your method is suitable. You can also use this reading to start writing your literature review – we always tell our students that you should always start writing as soon as possible. It's amazing how quickly time passes when you're working on your dissertation, so planning and time management are key.

Now you've chosen your methods, you can also start writing about them. You will need a 'Methodology and Methods' section in your dissertation, and you can start thinking about what you will write. Whichever method you have chosen, you will be able to find out more from books specifically focused on that method, and on the bigger research methods textbooks, which have room for more detail. This book is a starting point, but like all academic work, there's always more you can do, and the more you read, the better your work will be.

We hope you've found this book useful and that you're now feeling positive about the challenges ahead. Your dissertation is the culmination of all your hard work over the years and an opportunity for you to really show your supervisors and lecturers how well you can do. Go out there and impress them!

Good luck!

INDEX